# Financial Letters to Help Churches

# Financial Letters to Help Churches

## by
## Elizabeth Whitney Crisci

114 Bush Road • P.O. Box 17306
Nashville, TN 37217
Phone: 615-361-1221

All Scripture references are from the *King James Version*.

Cover Illustration: Ray Sanders
Cover Design: Keith Fletcher

Financial Letters to Help Churches
Second Edition

© Copyright 1990, 1997
Randall House Publications
Nashville, TN 37217
All rights reserved.
Printed in the United States of America
ISBN 089265-721-9

# TABLE OF CONTENTS

Editor's Preface
Introduction

Chapter One: LETTERS TO TEACH TITHING
1) A Message From God ...........................1
2) Praise God .........................................3
3) It's The Word .....................................4
4) No Argument .....................................5
5) Testimony .........................................6
6) A Verse To Remember ..........................7
7) Look Again .......................................8
8) God's Wisdom ...................................9
9) Just Old Testament? ...........................10
10) Moses' Example ................................11
11) Once Again ......................................12
12) Never Go Back ..................................13

Chapter Two: LETTERS TO HELP THE BUILDING OR
            IMPROVEMENT FUND
1) A Big Thank You ...............................15
2) Yes! We Can! ...................................16
3) Figure It Out ...................................17
4) One Nail At A Time ...........................18
5) Erase A Debt ....................................19
6) For God's Glory ................................20
7) Either Way .......................................22
8) Bible Thoughts .................................23
9) Perhaps! .........................................24
10) No Money, Please .............................25
11) It All Adds Up .................................26
12) Some Can Only Pray ..........................27

Chapter Three: LETTERS TO PROMOTE MISSIONS GIVING

1) Over The Sea .....................................29
2) Matthew 28:19 ...................................31
3) Map It Out ......................................32
4) Pennies Add Up .................................33
5) Missionaries Need To Eat .......................34
6) Over And Above .................................35
7) There's A Limit .................................36
8) Bless All The Missionaries ......................37
9) Missions Begin At Home .........................38
10) A Faith Promise ................................39
11) Let Others Give ................................40
12) Pray, Please ...................................42

Chapter Four: LETTERS TO ENCOURAGE STOREHOUSE
GIVING

1) Check The Word .................................43
2) Lord Teach Me ..................................45
3) But By Mail .....................................46
4) Why Not? .......................................47
5) Home Base ......................................48
6) A Worthy Workman .............................49
7) Cost Too Much ..................................50
8) God Is In Control ...............................52
9) It's Our Church .................................53
10) Remember The Past ............................54
11) Paul Said ......................................55
12) Floodgates .....................................56

Chapter Five: LETTERS TO FORMER GIVERS

1) You're Missed ...................................59
2) News To Pray Over ..............................61
3) Remember .......................................62
4) The Work Goes On ..............................63
5) If ...............................................64
6) God Is Still Here ...............................65
7) Same Place ......................................67
8) Praise God For You ..............................69

9)   Take My Life . . . . . . . . . . . . . . . . . . . . . . . . . . . . . . . . . . .71
10)  A Step Back . . . . . . . . . . . . . . . . . . . . . . . . . . . . . . . . . . . .72
11)  God Is Good . . . . . . . . . . . . . . . . . . . . . . . . . . . . . . . . . . . .73
12)  We Need Each Other . . . . . . . . . . . . . . . . . . . . . . . . . . . . .74

Chapter Six: LETTERS TO FUTURE GIVERS
1)   Never Too Young . . . . . . . . . . . . . . . . . . . . . . . . . . . . . . . .75
2)   How About You . . . . . . . . . . . . . . . . . . . . . . . . . . . . . . . . .77
3)   Try It . . . . . . . . . . . . . . . . . . . . . . . . . . . . . . . . . . . . . . . . .78
4)   Look Into The Word . . . . . . . . . . . . . . . . . . . . . . . . . . . . .80
5)   Now Is The Best Time . . . . . . . . . . . . . . . . . . . . . . . . . . . .81
6)   Have You Considered? . . . . . . . . . . . . . . . . . . . . . . . . . . .82
7)   You Are God's Child . . . . . . . . . . . . . . . . . . . . . . . . . . . . .83
8)   Think Ahead . . . . . . . . . . . . . . . . . . . . . . . . . . . . . . . . . . .84
9)   The Bible Tells Me So . . . . . . . . . . . . . . . . . . . . . . . . . . . .85
10)  Don't Forget . . . . . . . . . . . . . . . . . . . . . . . . . . . . . . . . . . .86
11)  The Reason Why . . . . . . . . . . . . . . . . . . . . . . . . . . . . . . . .87
12)  Begin Today . . . . . . . . . . . . . . . . . . . . . . . . . . . . . . . . . . .88

Chapter Seven: LETTERS TO FAR AWAY GIVERS
1)   Greetings From Far Away . . . . . . . . . . . . . . . . . . . . . . . . .89
2)   We're Still Serving . . . . . . . . . . . . . . . . . . . . . . . . . . . . . .90
3)   Don't Forget To Pray . . . . . . . . . . . . . . . . . . . . . . . . . . . .91
4)   You'll Never Know . . . . . . . . . . . . . . . . . . . . . . . . . . . . . .92
5)   A Blessing . . . . . . . . . . . . . . . . . . . . . . . . . . . . . . . . . . . . .93
6)   A Note To Inform You . . . . . . . . . . . . . . . . . . . . . . . . . . .94
7)   Praise To The Savior . . . . . . . . . . . . . . . . . . . . . . . . . . . . .95
8)   You Are Special . . . . . . . . . . . . . . . . . . . . . . . . . . . . . . . .96
9)   We Hear . . . . . . . . . . . . . . . . . . . . . . . . . . . . . . . . . . . . . .97
10   God's Added Blessings . . . . . . . . . . . . . . . . . . . . . . . . . . .98
11)  Sincere Thanks . . . . . . . . . . . . . . . . . . . . . . . . . . . . . . . . .99
12)  Keep In Touch . . . . . . . . . . . . . . . . . . . . . . . . . . . . . . . .100

Chapter Eight: LETTERS TO MAKERS OF WILLS
1)   The Law Says . . . . . . . . . . . . . . . . . . . . . . . . . . . . . . . . .101
2)   We Must . . . . . . . . . . . . . . . . . . . . . . . . . . . . . . . . . . . . .103
3)   Some Wait Too Long . . . . . . . . . . . . . . . . . . . . . . . . . . .104
4)   Check The Word . . . . . . . . . . . . . . . . . . . . . . . . . . . . . .105
5)   Keep On Giving . . . . . . . . . . . . . . . . . . . . . . . . . . . . . . .107

| | | |
|---|---|---|
| 6) | It's Easy | 108 |
| 7) | Neglect Not your Family | 110 |
| 8) | Neglect Not God's Work | 111 |
| 9) | Consider Others | 113 |
| 10) | It's Possible | 114 |
| 11) | Not Just The Wealthy | 115 |
| 12) | Me? | 117 |
| Conclusion | | 119 |

# Editor's Preface

It is no surprise that *Financial Letters To Help Churches* flowed from the computer of Elizabeth Whitney Crisci. Her previous publications produced by Randall House Publications have enjoyed a rather wide distribution. They were *Letters That Help Churches Grow* and *Evangelistic Letters For Believer's Use*.

Mrs. Crisci has been prolific in her writing as she has been published by several different publishing houses.

*Financial Letters To Help Churches* comes from one who has had wide and extensive experience as a pastor's wife. Her letters are pointed, personal, and practical. They do not beg nor are they demeaning to the recipient but rather are encouraging and uplifting.

The ample Scripture references instruct, educate, coach, thank, and inspire the recipients to a higher spiritual plane of giving.

These letters are so constructed that they lend themselves to change, adaptation, or even to be mailed as they are. There are no denominational references in them making them accessible to any church or denomination.

I commend them to you and you to the grace of our Lord Jesus Christ.


RANDALL HOUSE PUBLICATIONS
Keith Fletcher
Editor-in-Chief

# INTRODUCTION

"FINANCIAL LETTERS TO HELP CHURCHES" is written to help a busy pastor, church secretary, and/or the finance committee to encourage the believers in a local fellowship to give: give more than they have been giving, to tithe and give an offering for the Lord's work at home and around the world.

It would be wonderful if everyone tithed in our churches and gave a substantial offfering besides. Our churches would be fully funded, our missionaries would be over-supported, and our pastors would all make a living wage.

But not everone is willing to give to the Lord over and above a quarter, or a dollar. Some feel very generous if they place a five-dollar bill in the offering plate. But what is that when their weekly salary might be $450.00 per week or even more? And let the pastor and church leaders lead by example!

Remember what God said:

**"How that in a great trial of affliction the abundance of their joy and their deep poverty abounded unto the riches of their liberality. For to *their* power, I bear record, yea, and beyond *their* power they were willing of themselves; Praying us with much intreaty that we would receive the gift, *and take upon us* the fellowship of the ministering of the saints. And *this they did*, not as we hoped, but first gave their own selves to the Lord, and unto us by the will of God"** (2 Corinthians 8:2-5)

Wow! God can and will work when people give themselves to the Lord. Then, their money flows easily into the church treasuries and on to the missionary needs.

Wow! If only our people would believe and do this.

This book is written to encourage people to GIVE, as God GAVE:

**"For God so loved the world, that he gave his only begotten Son, that whosoever believeth in him should not perish, but have everlasting life"** (John 3:16).

Let us pray that as letters are written. . .not begging for money, but instructing our people in dedicated Christian giving. . .that people will open their checkbooks, their pocketbooks, their wallets, and GIVE as

God wants them to. . .first having given their own selves.

Please, don't send every letter. Do not send a financial letter every week. But as the Lord leads, send a letter that meets the needs of your people where they are. Perhaps three or four letters a year, in different catagories, can be sent to the precious believers in your fellowship.

Always remember, more is gained by encouraging, thankful letters than begging, demanding, dunning letters.

Praise God if people learn to tithe and give an offering via some of these financial letters to help churches.

God bless you in your ministry.

Elizabeth Whitney Crisci

# CHAPTER ONE

# Letters to Teach Tithing

## 1) A Message From God

Dear Members and Friends,

You are a very special part of my life and that of our church fellowship. Together, we are working to spread the gospel in our community and around the world.

I am writing this letter to share a message from God. It is found in Malachi 3:10: "Bring ye all the tithes into the storehouse, that there may be meat in mine house, and prove me now herewith, saith the LORD of hosts, if I will not open you the windows of heaven, and pour you out a blessing, that there shall not be room enough to receive it."

Please, believe me: this is not a letter to ask for money. It is a letter to reveal a part of God's plan for our lives.

The American Heritage Dictionary defines the word T-I-T-H-E: "A tenth part of one's annual income paid for the support of a church."

Many can't see how they can afford to tithe. I declare, from personal experience, I can't see how I can afford not to. The more I give to God, the more He gives to me.

Tithing is a personal and private matter. I know not your income nor your giving, but I know God teaches us to give at least a tithe to Him. Why not experiment for one year and see how the "windows of heaven will open up to you?"

Thanks for reading this, and pray for leadership to consider God's best for your financial life. Lord willing, I will write again soon on this subject.

God bless you and keep you.

Pastor _____

*"Will a man rob God? Yet ye have robbed me. But ye say, wherein have we robbed thee? In tithes and offerings..." Bring ye all the tithes into the storehouse, that there may be meat in mine house, and prove me now herewith, saith the LORD of hosts, if I will not open you the windows of heaven, and pour you out a blessing, that there shall not be room enough to receive it" (Malachi 3:8,10).*

# FINANCIAL LETTERS TO HELP CHURCHES

## 2) Praise God

Dear beloved members and friends,

I praise God every day that He has allowed me to be the pastor of this loving and caring church. In the midst of my praise, I decided that I ought to share my praises with you, and you too can make your list of praises to our Savior.

I praise God that He saved me from my sins by the blood of Jesus.

I praise God for each new day.

I praise God for my family: my wife and children.

I praise God for my church family: each individual, young and old.

I praise God for supplying every need of mine.

I praise God for my health and strength for each new day.

I praise God for the ministry He has allowed me to have.

I praise God for my finances and His control over them.

I praise God that I can give to Him my tithe (a tenth of all).

I praise God for all the extras He supplies for me.

Isn't God good? Doesn't He do over and above what we ask and think?

I discovered long ago that the more I give to Him, the more He showers on me. I trust you are enjoying the same experience.

> "God is so good,
> God is so good,
> God is so good,
> He's so good to me."

Keep on with Him and praise Him every day.

Sincerely in the name of our blessed Savior,


Pastor _____

*"For God loveth a cheerful giver" (2 Corinthians 9:7b).*

# 3) It's The Word

Dear friends in the Lord,

Do you like to receive mail? I do. I am always pleased when a friend takes the time to write to me. I am writing today as your friend in the Lord as well as your pastor.

Not only is it my responsibility to preach sermons from the Word of God, but also to teach you about Christian living. From me, you need to hear about your prayer life, your moral life, your family life, your business life, as well as your financial life. It is important that believers pay their bills, that they live within their means...not in debt to charge card companies beyond what they can pay in 30 days or in debt to friends or family. In our financial life the only sane, the only successful way to get a hold on our money is to begin with giving to God. He will shower His blessings on us and will enable us to have more than we ever dreamed possible. I've proved it in my life, and many of you have also.

IT'S THE WORD. Remember the Words of the Lord in 1 Corinthians 16:2:

"Upon the first day of the week let every one of you lay by him in store, as God hath prospered him."

Sometime, when you are free for a few minutes, call me and share some of your blessings in giving to the Lord. It would thrill my heart.

Sincerely in Christ,

Pastor _____

*"Upon the first day of the week let every one of you lay by him in store, as God hath prospered him" (1 Corinthians 16:2).*

# FINANCIAL LETTERS TO HELP CHURCHES

## 4) No Argument

Dear friend,

I like to keep in touch with you from time to time. I am writing to tell you how much I appreciate you and how glad I am that you are a part of this fellowship.

Being a part of God's family, being faithful in worship, and being a good, loving servant of the Lord is what makes life worthwhile, happy, and successful.

Because people love and care for this ministry of our church, we are able to continue in the work God has called us to perform in our community. Gifts and tithes from God's people keep our doors open, our young people taught, the children instructed, and our adults growing in the Word and in usefulness.

We can't successfully argue with the Bible. There is NO ARGU-MENT when God speaks. And the Bible tells us: "And the LORD spake unto Moses, saying, Speak unto the children of Israel, that they bring me an offering: of every man that giveth it willingly with his heart ye shall take my offering" (Exodus 25:1,2).

Your continued share in the Lord's work is greatly appreciated. Keep on with the Lord.


Sincerely,

Pastor _____

## 5) Testimony

Dear special ones in our church,

I am writing to share with you today some thoughts from people who found God sufficient and enhanced their lives through their giving of tithes and offerings.

One friend of mine told how he gave a substantial gift to the Lord, even though his children needed shoes. Already on its way was a package of shoes sent from a relative.

Far away, a missionary told about giving her last penny to help a struggling church in Africa. The Lord blessed with a package of very special biscuits from home, along with other necessities.

I worried about a big bill to pay and wondered where the money would come from. I thought, perhaps I shouldn't give to the Lord's work. But I did. Meanwhile, God led a man to send an anonymous gift for the pastor at just the right time.

Remember the widow's mite? She gave all she had (Mark 12:41-44). And she is remembered forever because Jesus commended her.

The testimonies are innumerable, from far and wide! I like the words of Walt Whitman: "When I give, I give myself" (from "Song of Myself," in Leaves of Grass 1855-1892).

The Bible tells us in Jesus' own words:

"And he called unto him his disciples, and saith unto them, Verily I say unto you, That this poor widow hath cast more in, than all they which have cast into the treasury: For all they did cast in of their abundance; but she... did cast in all that she had" (Mark 12:43,44).

Isn't God good?

In Christian love,


Pastor _____

# FINANCIAL LETTERS TO HELP CHURCHES

## 6) A Verse To Remember

Dear ones,

I like to share letters with you dear people from time to time. Although I do preach to you on the Lord's Day, there are many other things we ought to think about. It would be nice to just drop in and talk, and I do that from time to time, but other times, letters serve a more lasting purpose.

Today, my heart is fixed on God's Word and the memorization of it. In Psalm 119:11, the psalmist reminds us:

"Thy word have I hid in mine heart, that I might not sin against thee."

Therefore,I recommend a program of hiding God's Word in our hearts. To know and to do is what God wants of us. There are many verses to learn. Verses on salvation: like John 3:16; Romans 6:23; John 5:24. There are verses of comfort like John 14:1-3; Philippians 4:6,7; and Psalm 23. To learn a verse try reading it several times, print it on a card, say a phrase at a time, say as much as possible without looking, and keep at it until it is hidden in your heart. Then review every day for a while, then every week.

This week, try one of these verses and watch the Lord work in your life and fill you with blessing as you obey its words:

"The blessing of the LORD, it maketh rich, and he addeth no sorrow with it" (Proverbs 10:22) and/or

"Bring ye all the tithes into the storehouse, that there may be meat in mine house, and prove me now herewith, saith the LORD of hosts, if I will not open you the windows of heaven, and pour you out a blessing, that there shall not be room enough to receive it" (Malachi 3:10).

Yes, these verses are pointing toward God's financial blessings, and don't we all need that today? I praise God for you as you attempt these verses of blessing. I'm repeating both of them along with you.

God bless and keep you.

Pastor _____

## 7) *Look Again*

Dear members and friends of our beloved church,

I was thinking today, when I sat down to write this letter to you...am I closer to the Lord today than I was yesterday or the day before? Am I growing? Are you growing? Not in weight and width (although it wouldn't hurt to lose a few pounds), but in spiritual height and stature?

Growing is important and necessary in our Christian lives: through diligent study of the Word, in prayer, in worship and fellowship, and in witnessing. We know that, don't we? I dare add one more category to the growth list: giving!

Some get upset when we talk about giving; but be sure, I'm not taking an offering. I'm not seeking a raise! No, I'm seeking growth in our Christian lives. Almost all believers who are growing in each of the above areas grow in their giving: via tithes and offerings.

The principle of tithing began in the days of Abraham. Jacob continued his grandfather's practice as recorded in Genesis 28:22:

"And this stone, which I have set for a pillar, shall be God's house: and of all that thou shalt give me I will surely give the tenth unto thee."

Of course, this is Old Testament teaching, and it is not found in the New Testament. But cheerful giving is. Remember, the Ten Commandments are not listed in the New Testament as such, but Jesus summed them up. He did not say, "Thou shalt not kill," but He said in stronger language,

"Ye have heard that it was said by them of old time, Thou shalt not kill; and whosoever shall kill shall be in danger of the judgment: But I say unto you, That whosoever is angry with his brother without a cause shall be in danger of the judgment" (Matthew 5:21,22).

The Old Testament principle of the tithe is not the last word for giving, but the beginning for God's children. If you are growing in your faith, you will be growing in your giving. Examine your life and ask God to speak to you in any and every area where growth is needed.

Thank you for reading. Keep praying for each other.

Pastor _____

FINANCIAL LETTERS TO HELP CHURCHES 9

## 8) God's Wisdom

Dear friends of _____ Church,

We all need GOD'S WISDOM. It is found in God's Word; it is all true and precious. "All scripture is given by inspiration of God, and is profitable for doctrine, for reproof, for correction, for instruction in righteousness." Even verses concerning tithing are inspired by God.

We can begin way back in Genesis 14:20, "And blessed be the most high God, which hath delivered thine enemies into thy hand. And he gave him tithes of all." Do make a study of tithing. Tithing is the fairest way to give: Those with more can give more; those with less can give less.

Please, look up the following references: Genesis 28:22; Leviticus 27:30; 2 Chronicles 31:5; and Malachi 3:8–12. And remember, generous giving is a principle set forth in Scripture.

Be assured, I have no way of knowing how much you give, only the total of the offerings that come in. I realize that some give more than a tithe and others give much less.

Please pray with me that God's people in this congregation will pay a tithe and give an offering. God bless you and yours.

Sincerely in Christ,


Pastor _____

## 9) Just Old Testament?

Dear friend in Christ,

Greetings in the name of the Lord Jesus Christ. You are very special to me, and that is why I am writing to you at this time.

It has come to my attention that a few people (not necessarily you) in our church family think that tithing is old-fashioned, legalistic, and not meant for today. Let me share with you some Scripture.

It is in Malachi 3:10 that we read the strongest verse about tithing: "Bring ye all the tithes into the storehouse, that there may be meat in mine house, and prove me now herewith, saith the LORD of hosts, if I will not open you the windows of heaven, and pour you out a blessing, that there shall not be room enough to receive it."

Many Old Testament laws are not meant to be followed today. The sacrifices are gone because Jesus made the ultimate sacrifice on the cross of Calvary. The feast days are not necessary, but "Thou shalt not commit adultery" (Exodus 20:14) is very much in vogue. The world doesn't think so, but God's people do!

Jesus summed up the law in Matthew 22:37-40: "Jesus said unto him, Thou shalt love the Lord thy God with all thy heart, and with all thy soul, and with all thy mind. This is the first and great commandment. And the second is like unto it, Thou shalt love thy neighbour as thyself. On these two commandments hang all the law and the prophets."

My conclusion from this passage is that if we love the Lord as much as He requires in Matthew 22, we will want to give a tithe plus more of our income to Him. Think of that seriously: Giving is just one expression of our love for God and our neighbor!

I do not know the tithers from the non-tithers, unless you have shared with me your testimony in this area. I never see the financial books.

Thanks for considering the lesson of this letter sent in Christian love.

Sincerely in Christ,

Pastor _____

# FINANCIAL LETTERS TO HELP CHURCHES

## 10) Moses' Example

Dear church family,

It is good to keep in touch. Even though we see each other on Sundays and during the week at services, those occasions are limited in conversation and time. So, once in a while, I like to drop you a line to chat with you about my concerns.

Today's concern, stemming from remarks I overheard one day, concerns tithing. Many of you do tithe (give 10% of your income to the Lord), but some declare that it is an Old Testament teaching and we are no longer under the law. But we don't give up all the Old Testament laws like: "Thou shalt not steal" and "Thou shalt not commit adultery." And I believe that Old Testament tithing is not a command in the New Testament but just an example, a beginning of our giving experience. We need to use it as only a start to our dedicated contributions to the Lord's work.

Moses declared the words of the Lord to the Children of Israel:

"And all the tithe of the land, whether of the seed of the land, or of the fruit of the tree, is the LORD's: it is holy unto the LORD" (Leviticus 27:30).

Moses believed in, practiced, and taught tithing.

What more can we do? Let us follow his humble example; let us seek the Lord's will and give because that money belongs to the Lord. If we all give tithes, plus an offering, we would never have to mention giving again!

Thank you for reading this, and remember, we love you in the Lord, no matter what your stand is on tithing!

Sincerely and lovingly,


Pastor _____

# 11) Once Again

Dear ones in Christ,

Once again, I am writing to you special people in my life. As your pastor, I feel close to you: I pray for you, I'm concerned for you, and I enjoy your fellowship.

It thrills my heart to see the believers in this fellowship growing in their faith and Christian living. I am excited to see more of you increasing your commitment to the Lord. It is evident in your faithfulness at church services (including prayer meeting), in your concern for others as taught in Galatians 6:2:

"Bear ye one another's burdens and so fulfil the law of Christ."

My heart overflows every time I hear some of you witnessing to your neighbors or relatives. My heart overflows every time I see you enter the Lord's house for worship and fellowship. My heart overflows once again when I hear about God's people faithfully giving their tithes and offerings here at the church: to meet the needs of this body of believers as well as a strong missionary program.

Keep up the good work: not to make my heart overflow (as it does), but to please the Lord and bring glory to Him.


Sincerely in our wonderful Savior,


Pastor _____


*"...He that giveth, let him do it with simplicity" (Romans 12:8).*

# FINANCIAL LETTERS TO HELP CHURCHES

## 12) Never Go Back

Dear members and friends of _____ Church:

"Grace be to you, and peace, from God our Father, and from the Lord Jesus Christ" (Ephesians 1:2).

You dear ones are constantly in my thoughts and on my prayer list. I love you in the Lord and rejoice when I see you loving the Lord and living for Him.

I cannot understand how some believers fall away, turn from the Lord, get caught up in worldly activities, and no longer live a committed life. May I admonish you: Never go back to the old ways.

"Let us hold fast the profession of our faith without wavering; (for he is faithful that promised)" (Hebrews 10:23).

We cry when we hear of those who fall by the wayside. But remember, it begins with little things: getting away from the reading of God's Word, the Bible, forgetting the prayer life, not getting together with God's people for worship and fellowship, not giving to the Lord what belongs to Him (a tithe and an offering). If you see yourself falling back in a little area, seek forgiveness of the Lord quickly, and step right back into your dedicated Christian life before Satan grabs a hold on you and you can't get away easily.

God bless you as you live for Him. Never go back to the old ways, but daily submit your life to the Lord Jesus Christ. God has a task for you to do in His kingdom. It does not include backsliding. NEVER GO BACK.

God bless you in this endeavor.

Sincerely,

Pastor _____

> **"And Jesus said unto him, No man, having put his hand to the plough, and looking back, is fit for the kingdom of God"**
> **(Luke 9:62).**

## CHAPTER TWO

# Letters to HelpThe Building or Improvement Fund

### 1) A Big Thank You

Dear _____ ,

Praise the Lord, God's people have been giving for our needs in the building fund of our new (or improved) church building. What a difference it makes in the conveniences and the beauty of our worship area.

Although we know the church is the body of believers, we know that it is important to have the best possible building to attract unbelievers, to meet the needs of our youth and adults, and to draw our attention from the world as we meet with our God.

Each penny and dollar given for this fund has gone directly into this building, and we are so thankful for each individual who has made this possible.

Keep up the good work until the job is complete and we can publicly have a service of victory.

Your love in giving encourages me as your pastor and as your friend in Christ.

Sincerely in His name,

Pastor _____

*"My God shall supply all your need according to his riches in glory by Christ Jesus" (Philippians 4:19).*

## 2) Yes! We Can

Dear friend of _____ Church,

It is with great joy that I write to you today and share my delights and my concerns with you. Of course, I would rather sit in your home and discuss these matters, but since I can't get to every home, I can write to each of you.

My delights include the increased attendance in Sunday School, the commitment of those who faithfully come to our mid-week prayer meeting, and the new families who are joining us in worship. I praise God for our dedicated teachers, our spiritual deacons, and for the blessing you personally have been to me. People at our church make a pastor's work so enriching. Without you dear people, I could not carry on.

My concerns are for our building fund. With the increased activity and new people, I long to see our facilities spruced up and some new equipment added. We need a new copier, a commercial size stove, and a larger VCR screen. This work will come to over $8,000.00. Can we accomplish this? YES! WE CAN!!!!

YES! God can supply over and above what we ask or think. I pray and ask you to pray that many of our dear people will give a one time gift, over and above their present commitments, toward this special need.

Please pray with me, consider what you can do, and if possible, please offer to help in cleaning, painting, or whatever you can do to keep the price down.

Thank you from the bottom of my heart. You may use the enclosed envelope for your gift or the promise of a gift.

Let me share a verse of Scripture with you:

"This is a faithful saying, and these things I will that thou affirm constantly, that they which have believed in God might be careful to maintain good works. These things are good and profitable unto men" (Titus 3:8).

God bless you and use you.
Sincerely in our Savior's name,

Pastor _____

# FINANCIAL LETTERS TO HELP CHURCHES

## 3) Figure It Out

Dear friends,

It is with great joy that I write to you today. I have prayed, along with our committee and our people at prayer meeting, and together, by the vote of the church body, we feel it is time to fix the steeple (or put in new carpeting, or paint the outside of our church, buy the land, or ?). With God's leading, we have gotten three estimates and have chosen the one that is not only the least in cost, but presented by the company with the best reputation.

The price of the work will be five thousand, two hundred and fifty dollars ($5,250.00). That is a good competitive bid and we are assured that it can be given easily by God's people.

Note: If ten people give $525.00 we will meet our goal. If twenty people give $262.50, we will meet our goal. If forty people give $131.25, we will meet our goal. If sixty people give $65.63 we will meet our goal. If everyone gives liberally, we'll meet our goal.

It is important that we keep God's house in good repair for His glory. We never want to bring shame to His name. This is important to our continuing ministry. If you can give an extra gift at this time, we praise God for it. If you can't give an extra gift at this time, we will trust God to enable you to give the next time there is a need. We love you and pray for you either way! Please pray for us.

Praise God and trust Him for the meeting of this special need.

In Christian love and concern,


Pastor _____


*God's Word says: "But lay up for yourselves treasures in heaven, where neither moth nor rust doth corrupt, and where thieves do not break through nor steal" (Matthew 6:20).*

# 4) One Nail At A Time

Dear friend,

What a great day to be alive. What a great day to be anticipating the Lord's blessing on our church. What a great day to know that He supplies our every need.

"This is the day which the LORD hath made; we will rejoice and be glad in it" (Psalm 118:24).

As you know, we are in the process of rebuilding our educational wing. It will take a lot of time, energy, wood, nails, and much more to complete the work.

And to complete the work, we will need thousands of nails and other materials. Therefore, we decided to ask people to give: one nail at a time. If people would give a dollar per nail and we could add up all our gifts to be twenty-five thousand (25,000) nails, we would have enough money to buy both the nails and the wood, as well as pay for the construction crew.

Keep your eyes open for the big jar in the front lobby of the church. It will hold 25,000 nails. We will put the nails into the jar as fast as the people give. When it is full, we will begin our building program. Please pray and give as the Lord leads. We can do it

ONE NAIL AT A TIME!

Thank you for your interest and prayers.

In the name of our Savior, Jesus Christ,

Pastor _____

*"As we have therefore opportunity, let us do good unto all men, especially unto them who are of the household of faith"*
*(Galatians 6:10).*

# FINANCIAL LETTERS TO HELP CHURCHES

## 5) Erase A Debt

Dear church members and friends,

Isn't it great to know the Lord and see His goodness showered upon us? Isn't it tremendous to see Him meet our daily needs in our homes and in our church?

It has come to my attention that we are in debt in our building fund. The deacons, the finance committee, and I are concerned about this. The church is paying interest each month to pay off the debt. To my understanding, that is a waste of the Lord's money. I believe, with the help of God's people, we could erase that debt and save hundreds of dollars every month on the interest as well as not owing any bank a principal amount.

Romans 13:8 reads,

"Owe no man any thing, but to love one another: for he that loveth another hath fulfilled the law."

Although that doesn't necessarily say we shouldn't borrow money, if we are sure we have the wherewithal to pay it back, it is an admonition to pay up if and when it is possible.

Could we erase this debt? I believe we can. It will require your prayers and my prayers. Plus, it will take my sacrificial gifts, and it will take your sacrificial gifts; but remember,

"For with God nothing shall be impossible" (Luke 1:37).

If you feel led of God to help us with this "ERASE THE DEBT" plan, please use the enclosed envelope provided for your benefit. Above all, please pray with us.

Sincerely in the Lord Jesus,


Pastor _____

## 6) For God's Glory

Dear friend of _____ Church,

Isn't it wonderful how God leads in our lives? He guides us as individuals and as a group of believers. We are His Church, the body of Christ.

We want our building to bring glory to God. Therefore, we are seeking funds of $100,000 to increase our outreach to our community. We need to add a Christian Education wing (or whatever the church is in need of). The church has voted to proceed as the special funds come in.

Now it is up to us as a body of believers and as individual Christians to dig deep and give as we are able. Some are able to give large sums of money. Others, just as dedicated, can give smaller sums. But we are all able to give something.

May I recommend a sample prayer as you ask God what you should do for this important project that will be for His glory?

Dear Heavenly Father, Thank You for Your salvation, for Your guidance and help in my personal life and in the life of the church you have brought me into fellowship with. Our church is very special.

There is a big financial need. I can't supply it all, but I can do a part. Please show me what I can give. Help me to be willing to sacrifice over and above my regular contributions, and may my gifts and those of fellow Christians supply the necessary funds for the new Christian Education wing. And may You, oh, God, use that facility to reach young people of our town.

You are so good: I trust You to touch all our hearts and check books. Thank You. I praise You for the answer to this prayer. In Jesus' name, Amen!

No one will force you to give, no one will check up on your giving, but we will all pray and give as He leads. You may give a gift or make a

FINANCIAL LETTERS TO HELP CHURCHES

commitment by using the enclosed envelope. God bless you as you pray and give.

Sincerely in Christ,

Pastor _____

*"Give, and it shall be given unto you; good measure, pressed down, and shaken together, and running over, shall men give into your bosom. For with the same measure that ye mete withal it shall be measured to you again" (Luke 6:38).*

## 7) Either Way

Dear friends of _____ Church,

I like to write letters. It helps to have some thoughts in black and white so that we can read and re-read them and pray over them. And this is one of those days, for I want you to think and pray through a situation.

There is work to be done at our House of Worship. The rooms need cleaning, painting, and refurnishing. It will take money to buy paint; it will take money to buy new tables and chairs. And it will take time and muscle to scrub the areas and put new paint on the ceilings and walls.

Can you help us? EITHER WAY? Some can give money. Some can give time. (Some can even do both.) It isn't hard work, and the committee will assign you a task that you can perform: not too hard, or too involved. But we need YOU to volunteer...EITHER WAY.

The Bible says:

"So built we the wall; and all the wall was joined together unto the half thereof: for the people had a mind to work" (Nehemiah 4:6).

How about it? Can we count on you to give or to work? EITHER WAY!!!! Or if you desire, both ways. Let us know.

God bless you in this endeavor.


Sincerely,


Your loving pastor

# FINANCIAL LETTERS TO HELP CHURCHES

**23**

## 8) Bible Thoughts

Dear people of _____ Church,

I'm writing again...to share with you some special Bible verses. I love the Word of God, and certain verses stand out as I read and study from day to day.

Psalm 37:4 is one of my favorites:

"Delight thyself also in the LORD; and he shall give thee the desires of thine heart."

You may want to memorize that verse, if you haven't done so yet. Add to it the third and the fifth verses as well.

Often we sing another one of my favorite verses, Matthew 6:33:

"But seek ye first the kingdom of God, and his righteousness; and all these things shall be added unto you." I pray that my life will be in accordance with that word from the Lord.

Haven't we all heard, read, and even memorized Philippians 4:19?

"But my God shall supply all your need according to his riches in glory by Christ Jesus."

In my life, in your life, we all have seen God work just as He promised in that precious verse.

And that reminds me: We have a need in our building fund. We praise God that we can build and make our House of Worship a very special place to bring people to hear the gospel. But the bills must be paid. I am praying and I trust you are praying; and as we pray, let us remember,

"But my God shall supply all your need according to his riches in glory by Christ Jesus" (Philippians 4:19 bears repeating).

If you can give a little extra right now, it would help us in this special time of need. Thank you.

Gratefully,

Pastor _____

*"Ask, and it shall be given you; seek, and ye shall find; knock, and it shall be opened unto you" (Matthew 7:7).*

# 9) Perhaps!

Dear friends,

PERHAPS! Yes, perhaps this is the time to get busy with our hands and our wallets. There is work to be done at God's House, and perhaps God has chosen us to be the means to do that work! What an awesome thought!

Our hearts are overflowing with gratitude to the Lord. At a recent business meeting, the church voted to go ahead with our building plans. PERHAPS we will see our building enlarged to serve our God and our Savior in a more effective way.

God's Word is our direction for living. Note, the Bible tells us, "Therefore, my beloved brethren, be ye stedfast, unmovable, always abounding in the work of the Lord, forasmuch as ye know that your labour is not in vain in the Lord" (1 Corinthians 15:58).

Keep on with the Lord. He is so good! Be praying much about your involvement in the coming building campaign.


Sincerely,



Pastor _____


*"For we are labourers together with God: Ye are God's husbandry, ye are God's building" (1 Corinthians 3:9).*

# FINANCIAL LETTERS TO HELP CHURCHES

## 10) No Money, Please!

Dear members and friends of _____ Church,

This is a strange letter. Believe it or not, I want to say, "NO MONEY, PLEASE!" Wow! When is the last time you got a letter like this one?

Yes! NO MONEY, PLEASE! I am writing, as your pastor, to ask you to help us with our building. It won't cost you a penny, but it will cost you time. And if everyone answers this letter affirmatively, we will get a lot of work accomplished, even though you will not have to give a penny. Our work, in dollars saved, will amount to hundreds of dollars. And then, we can all say with the psalmist,

"Let every thing that hath breath praise the LORD. Praise ye the LORD" (Psalm 150:6).

We need people to wash woodwork, scrape, sand, and paint.

We need people to come and feed the workers.

We need people who know how to repair furniture.

We need people who can empty cabinet shelves and drawers.

We need people who can use a screwdriver and hammer.

We need people who can climb a ladder.

We need people who are willing to scrub floors and stoves.

We need people who will come and say, "What can I do?"

There is a job you can do: yes, YOU. Yes, even YOU! Will you volunteer next Saturday and/or any afternoon next week? Some of us will be there to find just the right job for YOU.

Thank you so much for helping. We'll all be blessed by your cooperation and hard work.

Sincerely in Christ,


Your Pastor

*"We then, as workers together with him, beseech you also that ye receive not the grace of God in vain" (2 Corinthians 6:1).*

# 11) It All Adds Up

Dear ones in Christ,

How about an arithmetic lesson today? If one and one make two, if two and two make four, if four and four make eight, then this letter will make sense.

Our church needs $10,000 for improvements in our youth facilities. It could be raised by. . .

| | | | |
|---|---|---|---|
| •one person giving | $10,000.00 | = | $10,000 |
| •ten people giving | $ 1,000.00 | = | $10,000 |
| •twenty people giving | $ 500.00 | = | $10,000 |
| •fifty people giving | $ 200.00 | = | $10,000 |
| •one hundred people giving | $ 100.00 | = | $10,000 |
| •forty children giving | $ 1.00+ | = | ? |
| •and 996 adults giving | $ 10.00 | = | $10,000 |

Think it through: There are hundreds of combinations that add up to $10,000. We can do it, and each one can give as he/she is able.

The Bible says:

"But who am I, and what is my people, that we should be able to offer so willingly after this sort? For all things come of thee, and of thine own have we given" (1 Chronicles 29:14).

Ask the Lord what He would have you do to help us raise the $10,000 easily because every one of us can do something special.

God bless you.

Sincerely,


Pastor _____


*"The earth is the LORD's, and the fulness thereof; the world, and they that dwell therein" (Psalm 24:1).*

# FINANCIAL LETTERS TO HELP CHURCHES

## 12) Some Can Only Pray

Dear friends,

"This is the day which the LORD hath made; we will rejoice and be glad in it" (Psalm 118:24).

And it is a beautiful day: a day to praise the Lord, a day to serve the Lord, a day to enjoy for His glory. As I sit in my study and think about the work of the Lord here in this church the Lord has called me to, I am very much aware that without the faithful prayers of God's people, this work would come to a quick halt.

I am asking today that you pray.

PRAY for me as I prepare sermons that they will speak to needy hearts.

PRAY for the Sunday School teachers as they prepare their lessons for their classes.

PRAY for the deacons and trustees as they serve in very important capacities.

PRAY for the coming building project planned to modernize the kitchen (or _____). God can and will supply the needed funds and the skilled labor as we wait upon Him.

PRAY that our people will give to make the project possible.

PRAY that those who can only pray will not feel inferior to those who give. Their contribution is greater, perhaps, than those who only give. I would much rather have a people often on their knees than those who merely reach into their wallets.

There it is: a letter thankful for those who can only pray. Some of us can add gifts of money to our prayers; others cannot. But remember: "The effectual fervent prayer of a righteous man availeth much" (James 5:16b).

God bless you all.

In Christian love,

Pastor _____

# CHAPTER THREE

# Letters To Promote Missions Giving

## 1) Over The Sea

Dear _____,

It is with great joy that I write this special letter to our flock of believers. We are one in the Spirit, and we are dedicated to the advancement of God's Word, here in our community and over the sea and around the world.

Our church is involved in the lives of people both here and abroad. God has told us:

"But ye shall receive power, after that the Holy Ghost is come upon you: and ye shall be witnesses unto me both in Jerusalem, and in all Judaea, and in Samaria, and unto the uttermost part of the earth" (Acts 1:8).

We are doing just that. We are giving to our local work; we are giving to God's work here in our own city and in our own country. We also are committed to sharing our money with home missionaries and with missionaries who have gone over the sea to the uttermost parts of the earth.

Let me encourage you to KEEP ON giving, praying, and considering actually going to reach the lost. God has used us in the past. He is using our family of believers right now, but there is more to be done. We pray God will use us in the future to serve Him around the world. Let's keep up our missionary giving and encourage some of our people to go and spread the precious gospel of Jesus Christ.

We must work together toward the fulfillment of the Great Commission.

Sincerely in Christ,

Pastor _____

*"But be ye doers of the Word, and not hearers only, deceiving your own selves" (James 1:22).*

# FINANCIAL LETTERS TO HELP CHURCHES

## 2) Matthew 28:19

Dear friend in Christ,

Greetings in the name of the Lord Jesus Christ, the One who loved us, died for us, and rose again for us. Isn't He wonderful?

One of the important parts of my ministry is to further the work of missions, locally and around the world. I read, over and over again, Matthew 28:19:"Go ye therefore, and teach all nations, baptizing them in the name of the Father, and of the Son, and of the Holy Ghost." I memorized this verse many years ago, and it is the driving force in my life.

How about you? Are you sold on missions? Are you concerned about the spreading of the gospel here at home and around the world, to all nations? We participate when as individuals, and as a church, witness to our neighbors and friends, our work associates, and our family, and when we go as missionaries or send out missionaries to all nations.

No, our church can't go to every nation. We can only do a little; we can go and send. We can pray the gospel around the world.

Let us as a church consider increasing our missionary giving as we obey Jesus' words in Matthew 28:19. Let's never stand still, but always reach out more every year to greater heights of missionary endeavor. It takes you and me to accomplish His purpose of teaching all nations. Pray for your part, as I pray for mine.

God bless you as one of Christ's very own missionaries: via giving, sending, going, and praying.


Sincerely in Christ,


Pastor _____

*"Go ye therefore, and teach all nations, baptizing them in the name of the Father, and of the Son, and of the Holy Ghost" (Matthew 28:19).*

# 3) Map It Out

Dear fellow laborers,

It is with great joy and thanksgiving to God that I write you. I have just finished looking at my world map. I see that God has called us to share the gospel around the world, via our gifts to the missionaries we help to support.

We have missionaries in Africa, in Europe, in Asia, in South America, in Eastern Europe, in Central America, and in North America. What a blessing, to us and to the missionaries. I believe we are fulfilling the call from Acts 1:8:

"But ye shall receive power, after that the Holy Ghost is come upon you: and ye shall be witnesses unto me both in Jerusalem, and in all Judaea, and in Samaria, and unto the uttermost part of the earth."

Thank you for your faithful giving to missions. Your gifts enable us to continue to spread the gospel here and abroad. This church is a thrill to my heart as I think of the work for the Lord we have a part in throughout the world. I praise God for you every day.

Why not spread the joy of missions giving with those who have not seen the vision as yet? They are missing the opportunity to serve the Lord in needy places. Your testimony might touch other hearts to give, to pray, and some perhaps even to go!

The Lord is so good, and He causes your life to bless my life!

Sincerely in Christ,


Pastor _____

*"And he said unto them, Go ye into all the world, and preach the gospel to every creature" (Mark 16:15).*

# FINANCIAL LETTERS TO HELP CHURCHES

## 4) Pennies Add Up

Dear friends in Christ,

This letter is written to a very special group of people: the prayer warriors and the believers here at _____ Church.

Because we are a "MISSIONS" oriented church, because we are a "MISSIONS" praying church, because we are a "MISSIONS" giving church, we need to think about what God has called us to do for Him.

At present, we give for missionary work in many countries around the world. We praise God for you, the faithful givers; our ministry is spread worldwide because of your faithfulness in giving. But there is a young couple who desires to go to a new country, just now opened to the gospel. We feel led to help them go, but it would entail an increase in giving.

What can we do for them? Some of us can add a little to our missionary commitment; some of us who haven't started to give to missions can do so right now and get them on their way. Some who feel that we should build up the home base rather than give to work overseas can rethink that position.

We have seen God work. The more we give to others, the more we see funds come into our church treasury. We can't give too much. So, please pray to see if you can take on some of this new burden. Remember, PENNIES ADD UP! Just place the enclosed card in the offering plate on Sunday, telling how much extra you can give. It needn't be a lot; a little from many will multiply fast.

Thank you for reading; thank you for considering an increase in your weekly giving.

Sincerely,

The Missions committee and Pastor _____

*"His lord said unto him, Well done, good and faithful servant; thou hast been faithful over a few things, I will make thee ruler over many things: enter thou into the joy of thy lord" (Matthew 25:23).*

# 5) Missionaries Need To Eat

Dear faithful givers,

You are a great people of God. We love working with you for the advancement of the gospel here in our community and around the world.

I am saddened by the news, however, that our missionary giving is down this month. Some are out of work; they cannot give. Some have grown cold to the need of missions. But if we fail the missionaries while they are on the field, how will they eat? How will their bills be paid? How will they be able to continue their work?

Let us pray and dig deeper for a little while until those who are sick are able to give again; until those who are out of work will have jobs again. We know missionaries have to eat, just like we do!

"Ye have not chosen me, but I have chosen you, and ordained you, that ye should go and bring forth fruit, and that your fruit should remain: that whatsoever ye shall ask of the Father in my name, he may give it you" (John 15:16).

God bless you in your missionary giving!


In Christian love,


Pastor _____


*"Pray ye therefore the Lord of the harvest, that he will send forth labourers into his harvest" (Matthew 9:38).*

# FINANCIAL LETTERS TO HELP CHURCHES

## 6) Over And Above

Dear friend of missions,

Because you love missionaries, because you give consistently to missions, and because the Lord is uppermost in your life, I dare to write you a special letter to present an immediate and temporary need.

One of our missionaries has a special need. _____ needs to come home on an emergency furlough because of a health problem (or family problem or whatever the need is). He needs approximately $2,000 for the trip. Two other churches are helping him, but we need to do our share because we love him in the Lord, because we took on a responsibility when we promised to support him, and because we love the Lord and want to do what He wants us to do.

This would be over and above our regular giving, and it would be a one-time gift.

Will you please pray about this need and see what God would have you do? Then, if you are led to give, please give a special offering in an envelope marked for _____'s special need.

Galatians 6:2 tells us:

"Bear ye one another's burdens, and so fulfil the law of Christ."

God bless you and lead you in your decision.

Sincerely in our Savior's name,


Pastor _____

*"If ye fulfil the royal law according to the Scripture, Thou shalt love thy neighbour as thyself, ye do well" (James 2:8).*

## F) There's A Limit

Dear friend in Christ,

Would you believe, we are not asking for money. There have been many offerings in recent weeks, and there is a limit.

We would love to give and give again, and give until it hurts. Many of us have done just that. Others have not found that blessing yet. But at this moment, our missionary giving is up to what it ought to be, and the Lord has met our missionary commitments through you.

We never refuse offerings, especially for missions. But at present, just keep at your present level of giving and those serving the Lord on the mission field will get their gifts on time and completely.

This kind of letter thrills a pastor's heart. This kind of letter thrills the hearts of the missions committee. You have become a blessing to us all. Keep up the good work and praise God with us every day.

Now our responsibility is to pray much for those whom we help support. So keep giving, but more, keep praying. Why not join us this week at our prayer meeting and lay before the Lord united intercession for those on the missionary battlefields of the world.

The Bible tells us: "Praise ye the LORD: for it is good to sing praises unto our God; for it is pleasant; and praise is comely" (Psalm 147:1).

With love and thankfulness,


Pastor _____
and the Missions Committee

# FINANCIAL LETTERS TO HELP CHURCHES

## 8) Bless All The Missionaries

Dear friend of missionaries,

How wonderful it is to be partners with our missionary family. How we praise God that we can be a part of the Great Commission via those we help send to Africa, to Europe, to South America, and around the world.

You are a vital link between their dedicated service and their means to get there and stay on the field. Sometimes they are in dangerous places, and there are many enemies to the Lord's work. They need our gifts, yes! But they need our prayers as much or more.

Too many people just pray, "God bless the missionaries." Because of our gifts, because of our communications from our missionaries, I trust we discover their needs and pray specifically for their individual concerns and needs.

Thank you...because of your faithfulness. We know God will bless the missionaries. Your continued contributions to missions make it possible. Your continued prayer sustains them in the battlefield for the Lord.

God bless you in His vital work of missions. Remember the Bible verse:

"Ask of me, and I shall give thee the heathen for thine inheritance, and the uttermost parts of the earth for thy possession" (Psalm 2:8).

Sincerely,

Pastor _____

*"And this gospel of the kingdom shall be preached in all the world for a witness unto all nations; and then shall the end come" (Matthew 24:14).*

## 9) Missions Begin At Home

Dear special people at _____ Church,

We, the missions committee, are writing a special letter to a special people with a special message: Missions begin at home!

Yes! Even though we spread our message around the world, even though our emphasis is often for the overseas missionary, we must not neglect those who work right here at home.

We have a project that we wish to bring before you for your consideration. There is a local work here among young people (or whatever the local need may be), and we feel it is important that we help the organization reach out to the needy and lost young people in this area.

What can we do? They have two requests:

1) that we pray for the workers and the programs they plan and 2) that we make a monthly contribution to their work.

Can we help? We as a committee have already decided that we would pray for this organization. Now we will bring a special request before the business meeting next week (or month) recommending that we give $25.00 (or whatever amount) a month toward this new and vital work. Will you make an effort to be at that meeting and voice your opinion? And, if the church votes to take on a monthly contribution, will you try to give a little more each month to help in this new project?

Thank you for reading and thank you for praying and acting.

Sincerely in the Lord's work,

The Missions Committee

*"And that repentance and remission of sins should be preached in his name among all nations, beginning at Jerusalem" (Luke 24:47).*

# FINANCIAL LETTERS TO HELP CHURCHES

## 10) A Faith Promise

Dear lover of souls,

I appreciate the opportunity to keep in touch with this wonderful congregation via personal contacts and via occasional letters. This letter is to help us all in the area of A FAITH PROMISE.

A faith promise is giving to God, not from our abundance, not from a large bank account, but from total dependence upon the Lord. We ask our people to give more to our missions program, over and above their church commitments, beyond what they give already, beyond what they can imagine.

"But," you say, "I have too many bills to give to missions. My family needs every penny." If we promise God that we will give a certain amount, He will supply it in a miraculous way. Make a faith promise and prove it.

One family made a faith promise when their children needed shoes. A bag of almost new shoes arrived the next day (the right sizes).

Oswald J. Smith had no money in the bank, a salary of $25.00 per week, when God led him to make a faith promise of $50.00 for the year for missions. He did, and at the end of the year, he was able to pay every monthly installment. Today, People's Church, which he pastored, gives in the millions every year to missions, following Oswald J. Smith's example.

It isn't a FAITH PROMISE when we promise to give out of our abundance; that is merely a promise. A FAITH PROMISE is to give God what we don't have, and we trust God to send in the extra to meet that need. He does. This church will never ask you to make up your FAITH PROMISE. You give as the Lord blesses and enables. Why not make your faith promise today!

Sincerely in faith,


Pastor _____

## 11) Let Others Give

Dear Christian friends,

My prayer for you is that you are growing in Christ, loving and serving Him, thus making your home and work life happier and better.

The Bible says,

"It is like a grain of mustard seed, which, when it is sown in the earth, is less than all the seeds that be in the earth: But when it is sown, it groweth up, and becometh greater than all herbs, and shooteth out great branches; so that the fowls of the air may lodge under the shadow of it" (Mark 4:31, 32).

We need to realize that we are a small church, and can't give a lot of money (as some people reckon) for the work of missions. We do give a high percentage of our tithes and offerings to missions; but in comparison to some large churches, it is only a little.

But remember the great hymn by Kettie Suffield: "LITTLE IS MUCH WHEN GOD IS IN IT, LABOR NOT FOR WEALTH OR FAME, THERE'S A CROWN AND YOU CAN WIN IT, IF YOU'LL GO IN JESUS' NAME."

Some say, "Let others give," and "Our little contributions won't make any difference." But I dare say to you, our little contributions and those of other small churches end up as big contributions and keep the missionaries on the mission fields of the world.

So keep praying, keep giving, and keep serving. May I paraphrase a famous president: "GOD MUST LOVE THE SMALL CHURCHES, BECAUSE HE MADE SO MANY OF THEM!"

We cannot sit back and let others do all the giving. God has told us to take the gospel to the ends of the earth. God said,

"And the gospel must first be published among all nations" (Mark 13:10).

Praise God for the church we are. Praise Him that we are a part of His missionary program. Never forget the words of Psalm 150:6:

# FINANCIAL LETTERS TO HELP CHURCHES

41

"Let every thing that hath breath praise the LORD. Praise ye the LORD."

We can't let others do the entire task; it is our responsibility too.

Sincerely,


Pastor _____

# 12) Pray, Please

Dear praying friends,

This is a prayer letter. Not a prayer letter from a missionary, as such, but a prayer letter from your pastor.

The missions treasurer has told me that we are behind in missionary giving. That saddens me, it saddens the Lord, it saddens our church, and it saddens the missionaries who depend on our faithful giving to keep them on the field.

But God has told us,

"He shall call upon me, and I will answer him: I will be with him in trouble; I will deliver him, and honour him" (Psalm 91:15).

So, let us wait upon the Lord and trust Him to meet this need. Please, spend specific time in prayer just for this special need in missions.

If our people won't pray and give, God will give the blessing to someone else: we will miss God's best. So PLEASE pray for us; now and each day, until the answer comes!

Thank you in the name of our prayer-answering God,

Your praying pastor,

*"And it shall come to pass, that before they call, I will answer; and while they are yet speaking, I will hear" (Isaiah 65:24).*

# CHAPTER FOUR

# Letters To Encourage Storehouse Giving

## 1) Check The Word

Dear Ones,

God is so good. He has blessed us as individuals, and He has blessed us as a church. He has fulfilled His promise in Philippians 4:19:

"But my God shall supply all your need according to his riches in glory by Christ Jesus."

Most believers love to give. They give to their family because they love them. They give to their neighbors when there is a need. They give to their church because of their love for the Lord Jesus. They give to many other Christian organizations because they sense needs around the world.

Our church has provided a way for you to give to the local ministry as well as to needs around the world. We recommend that our people give their tithes here in their local church and by the leading of the Lord. The vote of God's people divides between local church needs and missions.

If we share our tithe to appeals outside our local fellowship, our own church will not be able to carry on the work that God has called us to perform. Pray with us that our people will see the instruction of the

Lord in Malachi 3:10 about "storehouse" tithing. We can trust our dedicated boards to send our money around the world where it is needed.

Keep praying for each other. God bless and keep you in the hollow of His hand.

Pastor _____

*"Bring ye all the tithes into the storehouse, that there may be meat in mine house, and prove me now herewith, saith the LORD of hosts, if I will not open you the windows of heaven, and pour you out a blessing, that there shall not be room enough to receive it" (Malachi 3:10).*

# FINANCIAL LETTERS TO HELP CHURCHES

## *2) Lord, Teach Me*

Dear loved ones in the Lord,

Because I care for you, because I know you so well, because you are so precious to me and to the Lord, I desire to write to the dear saints in our church about certain matters that sometimes trouble me. Many of you are already doing what I think is the clear teaching of God's Word. Therefore, let this letter be an encouragement to you to continue in the way of the Lord. Some seem sure what God's will is for their life in some areas.

I'm writing to help you in one important area. I will leave the results with God and with you as you seek His wisdom.

Many give their tithes and offerings. They know that is what God wants them to do. Yet, they spread it out so thin: between the church, the charitable organizations in our community, missionary organizations, evangelists, TV preachers, and needy relatives.

I proclaim, from the Word of God, that we ought to bring our tithes and offerings into the storehouse: the local church.

The Bible says,

"Bring ye all the tithes into the storehouse, that there may be meat in mine house, and prove me now herewith, saith the LORD of hosts, if I will not open you the windows of heaven, and pour you out a blessing, that there shall not be room enough to receive it" (Malachi 3:10).

I am trying to instruct you in the way of the Lord. God will meet our needs, one way or another. If all our people practiced storehouse tithing, every need would be supplied, and we could give to many more projects where we see a need.

Please, pray "LORD, TEACH ME" concerning this matter. Trust the Lord as you bring your tithes into the storehouse; and then, as the Lord blesses you with His open windows, you can give over and above to other organizations if He so leads.

Thank you for considering God's Word.

Sincerely in Christ,

Pastor _____

## 3) But My Mail...

Dear ones at _____ Church,

I am writing to encourage you in a responsibility that has burdened my heart and those of our church boards. As believers we desire to serve the Lord in the best fashion possible.

Today, we are thinking about tithing. That can be a touchy subject. Some declare that tithing is following the Old Testament law rather than following the New Testament teaching of Christian liberty. We dare teach that tithing is a principle that we need not heed to the letter, but use as a beginning of our blessings in giving.

This letter is sent to talk about the practice of storehouse tithing!

What do we mean by storehouse tithing? We mean: bringing our tithes and offerings into our local church; both regular and missionary giving belong where we worship. As members of the church we have opportunity to vote on what it is spent for, and we can actually see God work through storehouse tithing.

Therefore, we ask you to pray and consider storehouse tithing like we read about in Malachi 3:10:

"Bring ye all the tithes into the storehouse, that there may be meat in mine house, and prove me now herewith, saith the LORD of hosts, if I will not open you the windows of heaven, and pour you out a blessing, that there shall not be room enough to receive it."

For the sake of our local church, our missionaries, and for pleasing the Lord, why not begin to practice storehouse tithing and gifts. If all our people did, we would never again need to ask for money! Praise the Lord.

In God's love,

Pastor _____ and chairmen of the church boards

> *"Then Hezekiah commanded to prepare chambers in the house of the LORD; and they prepared them, And brought in the offerings and the tithes and the dedicated things faithfully" (2 Chronicles 31:11,12a).*

# FINANCIAL LETTERS TO HELP CHURCHES

## 4) Why Not?

Dear faithful one in the Lord's work,

Praise the Lord for the way He is blessing the work here in our beloved church. God is so good. I see His hand on our people, on our services, and on our outreach. It is because of your faithfulness in prayer, in attendance, in giving, and in inviting others that makes this possible.

To add to our effectiveness, I would like to make a request as your pastor. I believe in and practice giving my tithe and offerings to the local church, and if there is more to give, I then consider giving to outside organizations and needs. I base my belief in this matter not only in the Old Testament, realizing that we no longer live under the law, but in the New Testament teaching of giving from our heart: joyfully as He has taught us.

"Every man according as he purposeth in his heart, so let him give; not grudgingly, or of necessity: for God loveth a cheerful giver" (2 Corinthians 9:7).

So, if you haven't already, WHY NOT try this storehouse tithing and see how God blesses? WHY NOT? Experience the joy of it. You will be so thankful to the Lord. And in the process, God will enlarge our church and our outreach: guaranteed, if we all follow this storehouse giving.

God bless you and keep you in the hollow of His hand.

Sincerely in His name,

Pastor _____

> *"Bring ye all the tithes into the storehouse, that there may be meat in mine house, and prove me now herewith, saith the LORD of hosts, if I will not open you the windows of heaven, and pour you out a blessing, that there shall not be room enough to receive it" (Malachi 3:10).*

## 5) Home Base

Dear members and friends,

We praise God for you and for your faithfulness here at _____ Church. You are a special blessing in my life. You make my ministry easier and sweeter. You remind me of the Scripture verse:

"I THANK MY GOD UPON EVERY REMEMBRANCE OF YOU" (Philippians 1:3)

I am writing to you today to encourage you. You are serving the Lord faithfully. I just want to share this burden of mine with you and ask you to seek the Lord's guidance in a certain matter.

I am writing from our HOME BASE of the gospel of Jesus Christ. God has called us to do the work of spreading His Word around the world. That requires good stewardship from God's people.

But God has provided a way: a system that would eliminate letters and/or extra offerings. God has given us a method of giving: found in the Old Testament, and sanctioned in the New Testament.

Jesus sounds a warning. Let me share with you His words in Matthew 23:23:

"Woe unto you, scribes and Pharisees, hypocrites! for ye pay tithe of mint and anise and cummin, and have omitted the weightier matters of the law, judgment, mercy, and faith: these ought ye to have done, and not to leave the other undone."

Jesus is telling the religious leaders, as well as us today, that we are not to give tithes to show off; but we should be filled with faith, judgment, and mercy. But, He continues, don't leave the other matter of tithing undone! Had Jesus not been a tither, the Scribes, Pharisees, and hypocrites would have ridiculed Him unmercifully.

Wow! That assures me to do storehouse tithing. That makes Malachi 3:10 worthy of my following (read, memorize, and practice it). I will bring my tithes and offerings into the HOME BASE: the store house. Will you follow in this vital matter? For our church to continue to reach out, our dear people must remember the HOME BASE.

Sincerely in Christ,

Pastor _____

# FINANCIAL LETTERS TO HELP CHURCHES

## 6) A Worthy Workman

Dear friends,

How I praise God for the way the people of our beloved fellowship give to the Lord's work. Many of you give sacrificially to this local work and to our missionary program. We often sing the doxology:

"Praise God, from whom all blessings flow;

Praise Him, all creatures here below;

Praise Him above, ye heavenly host;

Praise Father, Son, and Holy Ghost" (Thomas Ken).

How we praise God that we can give enough to supply a living wage for our pastor and staff. God's Word tells us: "The labourer is worthy of his reward" (1 Timothy 5:18b). How we praise God that we can have a substantial missionary budget and keep our missionaries on the field. How we praise God that we contribute enough in our improvement fund to keep our church in top notch shape. This is possible because the majority of you practice storehouse tithing. It takes continued "storehouse tithing."

We believe that Malachi 3:10 is a principle for New Testament giving, not a law but a method of giving. And we are thrilled with the New Testament verses that admonish us:

"But this I say, He which soweth sparingly shall reap also sparingly; and he which soweth bountfully shall reap also bountifully. Every man according as he purposeth in his heart, so let him give; not grudgingly, or of necessity: for God loveth a cheerful giver" (2 Corinthians 9:6,7).

Thank you for your faithful "STOREHOUSE TITHING." Thank you for your continued prayer support of this work of God. Thank you for your loving service in our church. You are a blessing to the pastor, to the church board, and to the Lord Himself.

God bless you as you continue this dedicated life style.

Sincerely,

The Finance Committee

## F) Cost Too Much?

Dear members and friends of _____ Church,

Greetings in the name of the Lord Jesus Christ.

Let me share with you that those who practice "storehouse tithing" find blessings so great upon their lives that they would never stop. Their lives are full, satisfying, and overflowing with blessings as promised in Malachi 3:10.

Those who declare tithing, especially "storehouse tithing," "COSTS TOO MUCH" have not practiced and/or have not stuck with it long enough to see the blessings.

I challenge those of you who fear to give your tithe into the local church to try it for one year. Test the Lord and see if He will not make a "storehouse tither" out of you!

Always remember, I do not know who gives tithes and who gives more or less. As your pastor, I pray for people to tithe, but the financial books are never shown to me. I keep an eye on the financial balances; I know when we are behind in giving and when we are ahead.

Be careful as you tithe and give an offering, for the Bible says,

"Take heed that ye do not your alms before men, to be seen of them: otherwise ye have no reward of your Father which is in heaven" (Matthew 6:1).

COST TOO MUCH? No, your budget can always be met via tithing: God supplies abundantly over and above what we ask or think. I've seen it COST TOO MUCH not to practice "storehouse tithing." I pray God will bless those of you who already tithe, I pray God will con-

# FINANCIAL LETTERS TO HELP CHURCHES

vict those of you who do not tithe, and I praise God for those of you who are willing today to start "storehouse tithing."

In Christian love,

Your pastor

*"Bring ye all the tithes into the storehouse, that there may be meat in mine house, and prove me now herewith, saith the LORD of hosts, if I will not open you the windows of heaven, and pour you out a blessing, that there shall not be room enough to receive it" (Malachi 3:10).*

## 8) God Is In Control

Dear precious believers,

Isn't it good to know the Lord and to trust Him? Life is so wonderful when God is in control. I praise God every day that I don't have to be the boss in my life, but I can let God direct and guide my actions, my thoughts, and my words. Of course, sometimes I get in His way; and then the trouble starts! Romans 12:1 and 2 must be uttered and re-uttered every day of our lives:

"I beseech you therefore, brethren, by the mercies of God, that ye present your bodies a living sacrifice, holy, acceptable unto God, which is your reasonable service. And be not conformed to this world: but be ye transformed by the renewing of your mind, that ye may prove what is that good, and acceptable, and perfect, will of God."

When that is our prayer and our desire, the next steps in life are easy. One such step is witnessing! Another step is serving in the local church. And last, but not least, is storehouse tithing (Malachi 3:10) allowing this church to function in the black without constant pleas for money. Let God be in control!

Let us do all that God desires to do in our lives; let us keep Him in control. Let us praise Him for the victories He gives us every day! God bless and use you.

Sincerely in Christ,


Pastor _____


*"And all they that were about them strengthened their hands with vessels of silver, with gold, with goods, and with beasts, and with precious things, beside all that was willingly offered" (Ezra 1:6).*

# FINANCIAL LETTERS TO HELP CHURCHES

## 9) It's Our Church

Dear family in Christ,

"Then the people rejoiced, for that they offered willingly, because with perfect heart they offered willingly to the LORD: and David the king also rejoiced with great joy. Thine, O LORD, is the greatness, and the power, and the glory, and the victory, and the majesty: for all that is in the heaven and in the earth is thine; thine is the kingdom, O LORD, and thou art exalted as head above all" (1 Chronicles 29:9,11).

This letter comes to you as a praise to God for your sacrificial giving to the Lord's work here in our church. You, the people of this congregation, believe in storehouse tithing; the offerings prove it. And they should, for it's our church. We need to support it with gifts of money that belong to God: to keep it going, to keep it witnessing, to keep it spreading the gospel around the world. Thank you for all your tithes and offerings as you bring them into this house of worship. We feel sure that you are experiencing the joy and blessing of the Lord as you do so.

"Every man shall give as he is able, according to the blessing of the LORD thy God which he hath given thee" (Deuteronomy 16:17). Tithing is the fairest way to give. It is according to the way God has blessed us. It is God's plan.

The faithfulness of God's people in this local church is tremendous. Keep it up. And if per chance you are one of the few who are missing the abundance of God's showers of blessing, start now. Give your ten percent (tithe) and your offering here in our collections for God's work at home and abroad. You will be amazed at the riches of financial blessing, of family blessing, of church blessing, filling your life.

God bless you in your continued ministry with your gifts.

Sincerely in Christ,

Pastor _____

*"Not my will, but thine, be done" (Luke 22:42b).*

## 10) Remember The Past

Dear supporters of our work here at _____ Church,

I am writing to thank you for your faithful support of this ministry. It is a thrill to my heart to see the work going forward because you give and back up your gifts with your prayers.

God is blessing beyond measure. Our bills are paid and even though my "thank you" is minuscule in comparison, God's "thank you" will last throughout all eternity. Yet I must commend you. Some of you are able to give a little. Some of you are able to give a lot. We trust all of you are able to tithe and bring that tithe into your local church.

Let's REMEMBER THE PAST: The Bible tells us in 2 Chronicles 31:10:

"And Azariah the chief priest of the house of Zadok answered him [Hezekiah], and said, Since the people began to bring the offerings into the house of the LORD, we have had enough to eat, and have left plenty: for the LORD hath blessed his people; and that which is left is this great store" (2 Chronicles 31:10).

God will bless you abundantly as you continue to bring your gifts into His house. Your love for God's work blesses and encourages me!

Sincerely,



Your pastor, _____

# FINANCIAL LETTERS TO HELP CHURCHES

## 11) Paul Said:

Dear members and friends,

Once again, it is my privilege to come into your home via this letter. I am thrilled with the opportunity to fellowship with you at services in church, at special programs, and in your home as the Lord enables.

We at _____ Church do pray for each of you on a regular basis. Our prayer is that your lives might be filled with joy, that you might be growing in your faith and in Christian commitment, and that your witness will be effective in the lives of others.

The Apostle Paul teaches us how to live the Christian life, how to avoid false teaching, how to share the gospel, and how to act as believers in Christ Jesus.

Here are a few teachings, written through Paul via the Holy Spirit:

"Therefore, my beloved brethren, be ye stedfast, unmovable, always abounding in the work of the Lord, forasmuch as ye know that your labour is not in vain in the Lord" (1 Corinthians 15:58). What a verse on how to live the Christian life.

Paul goes on to share an important principle with us:

"Upon the first day of the week let every one of you lay by him in store, as God hath prospered him, that there be no gatherings when I come" (1 Corinthians 16:2).

Here the apostle is setting forth several rules for giving.

First, set it aside: the best way is when the paycheck comes.

Second, the first day of the week, Sunday, is the time for giving to God. Does that not imply that where we worship God, the offering should be given?

Third, the gifts are according to how God has prospered the person. Doesn't that reflect our tithing a "ten percent" of our income, or even more, as God has provided for His people?

I trust you see God working in your life via 1 Corinthians 15:58 and 16:2. God bless and keep you.

In that charity,

Your Pastor

## 12) Floodgates

Dear brothers and sisters in Christ,

Our hearts are overflowing. The FLOODGATES are opened and God's blessing is evident in our lives, as individuals, and as a body of believers.

Why? Because we have seen God work in our midst since we believed, and practiced, and experienced the joy of Malachi 3:10. For God declared boldly, "...Prove me now herewith, saith the LORD of hosts, if I will not open you the windows of heaven, and pour you out a blessing, that there shall not be room enough to receive it." What a promise to those of us who obey God in a particular area of our lives!

Our homes are blessed, our pocketbooks are blessed, our bills are paid, our fellowship is blessed, our Sunday School classes are blessed, our church activities are blessed, our services are blessed, and our entire lives are so blessed we don't have room enough to receive it!

Why? Is it because we are so good? NO! Is it because we work harder than others? NO! Is it because we attend church regularly? NO! Is it because we have good jobs? NO! Is it because we are careful with our money? NO! It is a direct fulfillment of the verse we just quoted, minus the first phrase. Now, let us look at the rest of the verse:

"BRING YE ALL THE TITHES INTO THE STOREHOUSE, THAT THERE MAY BE MEAT IN MINE HOUSE [and then the promise], AND PROVE ME NOW HEREWITH, SAITH THE LORD OF HOSTS, IF I WILL NOT OPEN YOU THE WINDOWS OF HEAVEN, AND POUR YOU OUT A BLESSING, THAT THERE SHALL NOT BE ROOM ENOUGH TO RECEIVE IT."

# FINANCIAL LETTERS TO HELP CHURCHES

Wow! Is God good! We do what He says and He blesses beyond measure. Thanks for reading. PROVE GOD this week.

Sincerely in Christ,

Pastor _____

*"Then Hezekiah commanded to prepare chambers in the house of the LORD; and they prepared them, And brought in the offerings and the tithes and the dedicated things faithfully" (2 Chronicles 31:11,12a)*

# CHAPTER FIVE

# Letters To Former Givers

## 1) You're Missed

Dear _____,

Greetings in the name of the Lord Jesus. You have been a blessing in our lives, and we praise God for all you have done in the Lord's work.

We do miss you. We trust all is well with you and that you are growing in the Lord. We pray that God is using you. We continue to think of your generosity in the past and we dare ask the Lord to send you back to us with your presence, your helps, and your generosity.

I can't help but think of 1 Corinthians 1:4:

"I thank my God always on your behalf, for the grace of God which is given you by Jesus Christ."

God is blessing in His work here in our church. We praise Him for answered prayer. With sincere love, we ask you to come back and be a part of the ministry, not just with your finances, but with your life and your gifts.

God bless you and use you.

Pastor _____

*"Grace be unto you, and peace, from God our Father, and from the Lord Jesus Christ. I thank my God upon every remembrance of you, Always in every prayer of mine for you all making request with joy, For your fellowship in the gospel from the first day until now; Being confident of this very thing, that he which hath begun a good work in you will perform it until the day of Jesus Christ"*
*(Philippians 1:2-6).*

# FINANCIAL LETTERS TO HELP CHURCHES

## 2) News To Pray Over

Dear Mr. and Mrs. _____,

I am so excited about what God is doing. I just had to share with you the blessings.

We saw five of our young people go to the youth conference and two of them rededicate their lives to the Lord. Another one trusted Christ for the first time. Aren't they worthy of our prayers and love?

Our Sunday School is rejoicing with an increase in attendance as well as an increase in interest in the Bible. The teachers are excited.

Our fellowship is experiencing a closeness that only the Holy Spirit can produce. How we praise God for working among us.

Many people have been faithful in prayer and giving, and we commend this work to you for prayer and gifts as you see God in our midst. The blessings will just keep overflowing.

If I can be of any help to you, in prayer, counseling, or just friendly talk, let me know. I do pray for you and with you, and I beg your prayers for me as well.

God bless and keep you.

Sincerely,

Pastor _____

*"For we are labourers together with God: ye are God's husbandry, ye are God's building" (1 Corinthians 3:9).*

## 3) Remember

Dear friends,

Our church is going forward in the work of the Lord. Our task is to win people to the Lord and to help them grow in the Christian life. We are burdened for our neighbors, and we are burdened for the community. We are burdened for our nation. We are burdened for the world.

Our task is to present God's Word. That is what we are trying to do. If God speaks to your heart, perhaps you could remember our ministry here with some of what God has blessed you with.

Do you remember your blessings here at _____ Church? God has blessed your life via this fellowship over and over again. We pray that you will remember those blessings and praise God for them.

If God lays it on your heart, perhaps you can remember the Lord's work here in a tangible way. There are needs in our current account, our missions account, as well as our building fund. We believe God will encourage and bless you by it. Even more, we ask for your continued prayers as we serve the Lord in this mission field.

Sincerely,

Pastor _____

*"But this I say, He which soweth sparingly shall reap also sparingly; and he which soweth bountifully shall reap also bountifully" (2 Corinthians 9:6).*

# FINANCIAL LETTERS TO HELP CHURCHES

## 4) The Work Goes On

Dear friend of _____ Church,

We are thankful for your past and present participation in the work of the Lord here at our Bible preaching church.

God is still blessing His work. We have seen His hand on the life of our youth, our seniors, and our worship services. We praise God that He has His Word to keep us close to Him. We, by God's Holy Spirit, must live the fruit of the Spirit:

"But the fruit of the Spirit is love, joy, peace, longsuffering, gentleness, goodness, faith, Meekness, temperance: against such there is no law" (Galatians 5:22,23).

As we believers practice these, as we are faithful in each one, we will continue to see God work. Some of us were more faithful than we are today. Jeremiah realized that when God led him to write,

"Thus saith the LORD, Stand ye in the ways, and see, and ask for the old paths, where is the good way, and walk therein, and ye shall find rest for your souls" (Jeremiah 6:16a).

In times past, you were more involved, through service and giving. Now we ask you to remember your old path and walk in it. Some in Jeremiah's day would not, for the end of that promising verse goes:

"But they said, We will not walk therein" (Jeremiah 6:16b).

You are still in our prayers. We still love you in the Lord. You have been and still are a blessing to us and the congregation.

God bless you,

Pastor _____

## 5) If

Dear friends,

What a beautiful day. "BLESS THE LORD, O MY SOUL: AND ALL THAT IS WITHIN ME, BLESS HIS HOLY NAME" (Psalm 103:1).

We bless the Lord for His goodness in our individual lives. We bless the Lord for taking care of our families. We bless the Lord for His guidance in our church activities. We bless the Lord for the new families who are coming to church services. We bless the Lord for those who have recently received the Lord Jesus Christ as Savior and Lord. We bless the Lord for YOU!

Yes, for YOU! As an individual, as a part of our fellowship now and in the past. We bless the Lord for your past service in our church and also for your past giving. Thank you for your generosity in this vineyard of the Lord.

God has told us in Proverbs 3:9: "HONOUR THE LORD WITH THY SUBSTANCE, AND WITH THE FRISTFRUITS OF ALL THINE INCREASE." If we all follow that word from Solomon, we would not need to write any further letters or seek any more funds. Solomon also wrote in the sixth verse of the same chapter: "IN ALL THY WAYS ACKNOWLEDGE HIM, AND HE SHALL DIRECT THY PATHS." I believe that includes our devotional time, our recreational activities, our family life, our work, and our financial transactions including our consecrated giving to our church.

Thank you for reading and thank you for considering a renewal of your gifts to _____ Church. You have been a real help in the past, and we trust God will use you in the future of this ministry.

God bless you and keep you.

Pastor _____

*"And I said unto them, Ye are holy unto the LORD; the vessels are holy also; and the silver and the gold are a freewill offering unto the LORD God of your fathers" (Ezra 8:28).*

# FINANCIAL LETTERS TO HELP CHURCHES

## 6) God Is Still Here

Dear ones,

Greetings in the name of the Lord Jesus Christ. We here at
_____Church love and serve Him, our Savior and our coming
King.
"I will praise thee for ever,
because thou hast done it:
and I will wait on thy name;
for it is good before thy saints"
(Psalm 52:9).
Yes, God is still here in our midst at _____ Church. We see His
blessings every day. No, we aren't perfect. We have acknowledged that
we are merely sinners saved by grace (Ephesians 2:8,9). But, in spite of
our weaknesses, we see our strengths as we proclaim the gospel of Jesus
Christ.
We dare ask you to return to your former zeal in our church. You
may have been hurt by some action here, but as we forgive each other
and rededicate ourselves to the Lord, we see He is most important, not
ourselves and our feelings. Let us live by the words of Paul in
Philippians 3:13,14:
"BRETHREN, I COUNT NOT MYSELF TO HAVE APPRE-
HENDED: BUT THIS ONE THING I DO, FORGETTING THOSE
THINGS WHICH ARE BEHIND, AND REACHING FORTH
UNTO THOSE THINGS WHICH ARE BEFORE, I PRESS
TOWARD THE MARK FOR THE PRIZE OF THE HIGH CALL-
ING OF GOD IN CHRIST JESUS."
If we have hurt you, we again say we are sorry. We want to be a
blessing and a joy in your life. Let us minister to you as you minister to
us by your presence, by your service, and by your continued zeal. God

is at work here, and God will use you here if you are willing. We love you and pray for you.

Sincerely and lovingly,


Pastor _____

*"And Jesus said unto him, No man, having put his hand to the plough, and looking back, is fit for the kingdom of God"*
*(Luke 9:62).*

# FINANCIAL LETTERS TO HELP CHURCHES

## 7) Same Place

Dear friends,

I love the Bible. I love its advice, its instruction, and its praise of my God. For instance, Psalm 102:27,28:

"BUT THOU ART THE SAME, AND THY YEARS SHALL HAVE NO END. THE CHILDREN OF THY SERVANTS SHALL CONTINUE, AND THEIR SEED SHALL BE ESTABLISHED BEFORE THEE."

The God of the Bible is still our same God. Our church, where we worship the Lord, is still the same place. Yes, there are changes; some people come, some people go. Some have gone home to be with the Lord, and some have moved. Some have traveled to other churches. We are still serving the Lord in the same place. And we long to have you come to this same place and share your tithes and offerings here in this same place of worship. Consider what God can do through you right here in this lighthouse of the gospel.

Always remember, even though we change, we trust for the better and in a closer walk with the Lord, Jesus never changes. Read, re-read, memorize, and quote often:

"LET YOUR CONVERSATION BE WITHOUT COVETOUS-NESS; AND BE CONTENT WITH SUCH THINGS AS YE HAVE: FOR HE HATH SAID, I WILL NEVER LEAVE THEE, NOR FOR-SAKE THEE. SO THAT WE MAY BOLDLY SAY, THE LORD IS MY HELPER, AND I WILL NOT FEAR WHAT MAN SHALL DO UNTO ME" (Hebrews 13:5,6).

"JESUS CHRIST THE SAME YESTERDAY, AND TO DAY, AND FOR EVER" (Hebrews 13:8).

God bless you...as you consider this God who never changes. God bless you...as you consider returning to our fellowship. God bless you...as you consider the renewing of your support to this place of worship. You are wanted and needed.

God be with you in your decision.

Sincerely in Christ,

Pastor _____

*"Jesus said unto them, Verily, verily, I say unto you, before Abraham was, I am" (John 8:58).*

# FINANCIAL LETTERS TO HELP CHURCHES

## 8) Praise God For You

Dear ones in the Lord,

I praise God for you. Like Paul, I say,

"I thank my God upon every remembrance of you" (Philippians 1:3).

It has been good to see God use you in various ways. You have served on various committees and boards in the past. You have been involved in our Sunday School and church services. You have been generous in your giving to our church.

We realize that you were upset over a past problem. But we feel that has been resolved and God has worked in our lives. We have asked for forgiveness where we have not done right; we have sought peace among the brethren; we have trusted the Lord to bring healing.

We feel it is now time for us to unite in love and service and go forward together to reach the area and the world for Christ. Again, Paul wrote:

"I therefore, the prisoner of the Lord, beseech you that ye walk worthy of the vocation wherewith ye are called, With all lowliness and meekness, with longsuffering, forbearing one another in love; Endeavouring to keep the unity of the spirit in the bond of peace" (Ephesians 4:1-3).

If we follow that Scripture, we will all want to work together for God's glory. We pray that now you will be involved again, that you will pray with us, that you will make your talents and resources available to God, both of which are service to the Lord.

Thank you for reading and considering my letter. I love you, and the body of believers loves you in the Lord. Let us never forget the words of Jesus:

"Neither pray I for these alone, but for them also which shall believe on me through their word; That they may be one: as thou, Father, art in me, and I in thee, that they also may be one in us: that the world may believe that thou hast sent me" (John 17:20,21).

If we serve together in love and unity, the world will see Jesus and believe in Him.

God bless you as you pray about continued service here in our fellowship.

Sincerely yours in our Savior's name,

Pastor _____

# FINANCIAL LETTERS TO HELP CHURCHES

## 9) Take My Life

Dear friends,

Take my life, and let it be
Consecrated, Lord, to Thee;
Take my moments and my days,
Let them flow with ceaseless praise,
Let them flow with ceaseless praise.
Take my lips and let them be
Filled with messages for Thee;
Take my silver and my gold,
Not a mite would I with-hold;
Not a mite would I with-hold.
(Frances R. Havergal)

This hymn has been my prayer over and over again. I long to have it fulfilled in my life. When I sing it, I mean it. When I get out into the world, I sometimes forget it. My prayer is that this commitment may be a moment by moment desire of my heart. And then, with the power of the Holy Spirit, I can make it!

We praise God for your consecrated service in the past.

We pray now that you, by God's grace, will be able to continue your faithfulness in attendance, in working with us, and in giving. We cannot live on our past laurels, but we must do what the Apostle Paul taught us by his example:

"Brethren, I count not myself to have apprehended: but this one thing I do, forgetting those things which are behind, and reaching forth unto those things which are before, I press toward the mark for the prize of the high calling of God in Christ Jesus" (Philippians 3:13,14).

We need to forget what has hindered our service, whether our fault, or someone else's, and dig in again, remembering the hymn: "TAKE MY LIFE" and remembering the Scripture: "Forgetting...press toward the mark."

I pray with you as you re-commit your life to the Lord and His work.

Sincerely in Christ,

Pastor _____

# 10) A Step Back

Dear friends in Christ,

Greetings in the Savior's Name. We love Him and we love you.

The Lord is good. He has met our needs and blessed our people. It seems the more we give to Him, in time and money, the more He gives back to us.

We miss your labor of love and your gifts for this work. The psalmist gave us this word:

"O God, my heart is fixed: I will sing and give praise, even with my glory" (Psalm 108:1).

We all need to fix our eyes on Jesus, not on people, not even Christian people, not even on me as pastor. We all fail.

"Master, I will follow thee whithersoever thou goest" (Matthew 8:19).

The beloved chorus, written by an unknown writer, tells us:

I have decided to follow Jesus,
I have decided to follow Jesus,
I have decided to follow Jesus,
No turning back, no turning back!
The world behind me, the cross before me,
The world behind me, the cross before me,
The world behind me, the cross before me,
No turning back, no turning back!

Thank you for all you have done for God's work in the past. Thank you for what you are going to do in the future. I ask that you consider doing it again through our local church. We believe God is using this work for His glory. We believe His hand is upon our ministry. We feel God can use you right here in our midst. Thanks for all you've done with and through us.

Sincerely,

Pastor _____

# FINANCIAL LETTERS TO HELP CHURCHES

## 11) God Is Good

Dear _____,

This letter is written in love. This letter is written because of Jesus and His love...plus our love for you.

The work of the Lord must go on; it will go on. There is a command of the Lord,

"And said unto them, Thus it is written, and thus it behoved Christ to suffer, and to rise from the dead the third day: And that repentance and remission of sins should be preached in his name among all nations, beginning at Jerusalem. And ye are witnesses of these things" (Luke 24:46-48).

In times past, you have been very faithful to support this ministry at _____ Church. We are so thankful for every gift you gave. Through you, and others like you, we were able to reach our community with the gospel. Through you, we were able to expand our missionary program. Through you, we were able to beautify our house of worship. We understand that you have been hurt and that you have stopped your support.

This letter is written to ask you to consider beginning again, to resume your support to this fellowship, because there is a great work to do; we want you to receive the blessing, just as we are.

I ask that you forget the hurts and any harsh words, that you seek the Lord's will and humble yourself before Him. This letter is intended to encourage you. Please take it in the spirit it is sent.

We love you no matter how you decide. God loves you and wants to use you. Keep on with Him, no matter what.

God bless you and use you. You are in my personal prayers and in the prayers of the congregation.

Lovingly,

Pastor _____

## 12) We Need Each Other

Dear friends of _____ Church,

Imagine living alone...no neighbors, no friends, no family, or no human being around anywhere! Almost an impossible thought, certainly an impossible life style. WE NEED EACH OTHER!

Ephesians 4 guides us in the way we should act as a church. Read the entire chapter after you read this portion:

"I therefore, the prisoner of the Lord, beseech you that ye walk worthy of the vocation wherewith ye are called, With all lowliness and meekness, with longsuffering, forbearing one another in love; Endeavouring to keep the unity of the spirit in the bond of peace" (Ephesians 4:1-3).

We need each other. I need you. I have always appreciated your help in the gospel. The congregation needs your insights and labors. You need us as well. Once you were a contributor of time and money. You have backed away, and I am sure you felt you had good reason; but perhaps no reason is good in God's eyes. You need us just as much as we need you. Please, with longsuffering, forbearing one another in love, endeavoring to keep the unity of the Spirit in the bond of peace, try again. We will all be better off if we obey these verses!

Thank you for reading; thank you for praying about your re-commitment to this fellowship with your support and service. God bless you and use you in your decision. We'll keep right on loving you and praying with you, whichever way God leads you.

Sincerely in Christ,


Pastor _____

*"And be ye kind one to another, tenderhearted, forgiving one another, even as God for Christ's sake hath forgiven you"*
*(Ephesians 4:32)*

# CHAPTER SIX

# Letters To Future Givers

## 1) Never Too Young

Dear _____,

We are so happy that you are a part of our church. You are a sweet child and a blessing to one and all in our Sunday School and services.

We praise God for you and are thankful for your faithfulness and for the lessons you are learning about the Lord Jesus Christ. We pray that you have trusted Him as your Savior while you are young so you can live your whole life for Him.

One lesson we want you to learn, while you are still young, is to give your offerings to the Lord. The Bible teaches us to give a tithe: one tenth of all our income (Malachi 3:10). That means, if you have a dollar, ten cents of that dollar belongs to God. If you only have a dime, a penny of that dime belongs to the Lord. So, put your tithe, your tenth, into your church offering. Of course, always remember that God is pleased with an offering above your tithe. You could give fifteen cents out of your dollar, or more, if you want to. Pray about how much you should give to Him, and remember to be happy about your gifts.

The Bible says...

"For God loveth a cheerful giver" (2 Corinthians 9:7b).

We look forward to seeing you on Sunday. God bless you.

In Christian Love,

Your Pastor

*"Every man according as he purposeth in his heart, so let him give; not grudgingly, or of necessity: for God loveth a cheerful giver" (2 Corinthians 9:7).*

# FINANCIAL LETTERS TO HELP CHURCHES

## 2) How About You?

Dear _____,

Even though you are young, you are important to me. I pray for you and I encourage our Sunday School teachers and youth workers as they teach you in God's ways. Never turn from the Lord who loves you and gave Himself for you.

In this letter, I wish to help you in a special part of your life. God has encouraged everyone to put Him first in our activities, our thoughts and actions, our homelife, our life outside the home, and even in our giving.

We believe God wants you to learn to give while you are still young. You are able if you get an allowance, if you work occasionally, or if you get gifts of money. HOW ABOUT YOU? Can you learn to give?

YES! Every time you earn a dollar, set aside a dime for God.

Every time you earn ten dollars, set aside one dollar for God.

Every time you earn $25.00: give God $2.50.

It's not difficult. God will enable you to give if you so desire. And it is better to give from your own money than to ask your parents for money for an offering. It pleases your Savior.

The Bible says,

"Every man according as he purposeth in his heart, so let him give; not grudgingly, or of necessity: for God loveth a cheerful giver" (2 Corinthians 9:7).

You, as one of our precious young people, are very, very special to me and to our entire church.

God bless you in your giving and your living for the Lord.


Pastor _____

## 3) Try It

Dear young person,

What a wonderful age you are! What a wonderful time of life for you!

You are at a time in your life when you are beginning to make decisions. Decisions about who to have as friends. Decisions about your future career. Decisions about your beliefs! The most important decision you will ever make is to believe on the Lord Jesus Christ as Savior. The Bible says,

"...Believe on the Lord Jesus Christ, and thou shalt be saved, and thy house" (Acts 16:31).

Please, make that decision now, while you are young! Then you can avoid the pitfalls of sin that too many young people fall into.

And decide to live a godly, Christian life, according to Bible teaching. That includes a moral, loving life without stealing, cheating, swearing, pre-marital sex, and other sexual sins.

Decide while you are young to give your money and time to the Lord. Money? What money? Yes, your money. You have some: allowance, part- time job, gifts. God tells us to give a tenth (tithe) of our money to Him and to give it to the church. If you have $1.00 - give God 10 cents. If you have $10.00 - give God $1.00. If you have $100.00 - give God $10.00.

And even give more than 10% (tithe). If you start small, as a young person, then it will be easy to tithe (10%) when you are older and have more money.

Why not TRY IT! Why not experiment now: today! Give your tithe to your church. God will bless you and make you a blessing to others.

Come talk to me and tell me about receiving Christ as your Savior. Come talk to me and tell me about your experience with tithing! Come talk to me about any questions you may have!

# FINANCIAL LETTERS TO HELP CHURCHES

God loves you so much that He gave His only begotten Son to die for you (John 3:16). Never forget that!

In Christian love,


Pastor _____

*"Honour the LORD with thy substance, and with the firstfruits of all thine increase" (Proverbs 3:9).*

## 4) Look Into The Word

Dear friend,

The Bible says,

"Speak unto the children of Israel, that they bring me an offering: of every man that giveth it willingly with his heart ye shall take my offering" (Exodus 25:2).

God is good; God loves you; God knows everything; God sent His Son to die for you and for me.

"For God so loved the world, that he gave his only begotten Son, that whosoever believeth in him should not perish, but have everlasting life" (John 3:16).

You, as a young person, must come to God through Jesus. You must believe that Jesus died for you, that He rose from the dead for you, and that He is coming back for you. You must ask Jesus into your life and ask Him to forgive your sin and be your Savior, and then you are a true Christian.

And once you are a Christian, you should want to give to the Lord on a regular basis. You should give an offering to the Lord now! Don't wait until you are older. Do it now, out of your own money (rather than ask your parents for money for church). Get excited about your giving. See the blessings come into your life as you do what God tells you to do. Someday, you will be able to give larger sums, but in the meantime, give a tenth (a tithe) of what you have. You'll be pleasing the Lord and you will be thrilled with the results.

You are in our prayers and we praise God that you attend this church. Keep coming regularly. I am glad you read this letter. I trust you will learn the joy of giving, just like so many people in our church. God bless you in all you do.

Pastor _____

*"Every man according as he purposeth in his heart, so let him give; not grudgingly, or of necessity: for God loveth a cheerful giver" (2 Corinthians 9:7).*

# FINANCIAL LETTERS TO HELP CHURCHES

## 5) Now Is The Best Time

Dear young friends,

It's fun to get mail. It's great to read about interesting subjects. I am pleased you are reading my letter.

I would like to challenge you.

When you grow up, you will want to give to God's work.

I would like to challenge you.

Why not start giving NOW!

I would like to challenge you.

Now is the best time to start giving to God.

You are young; you are starting good habits in your life. Giving to God is a wonderful habit to establish while you are young. If you love God, if you have received Jesus Christ into your life as Savior, one way to show it is with your gifts.

God's Word, the Bible, tells us:

"If ye love me, keep my commandments" (John 14:15).

God's Word the Bible, says to us:

"Bring ye all the tithes [10% of what money you have] into the storehouse [the church]...I will...pour you out a blessing..." (Malachi 3:10).

Now is the best time to give: You can start small because your money is little, and you will see your gifts grow along with your blessings. People, young and old, who love God, want to give to Him. Keep loving Him and keep His commandments.

Lovingly,

Pastor _____

## 6) Have You Considered?

Dear Sunday School friend (Youth Group friend),

Have you considered believing on the Lord Jesus Christ? The Bible says:

"And they said, Believe on the Lord Jesus Christ, and thou shalt be saved, and thy house" (Acts 16:31).

Have you considered putting Jesus first in your life? The Bible says,

"But seek ye first the kingdom of God, and his righteousness; and all these things shall be added unto you" (Matthew 6:33).

Have you considered giving to God every Sunday via church envelopes? The Bible says,

"Upon the first day of the week let every one of you lay by him in store, as God hath prospered him, that there be no gatherings when I come" (1 Corinthians 16:2).

Have you considered praying every day? The Bible says:

"Pray without ceasing" (1 Thessalonians 5:17).

The Bible says:

"Praying always with all prayer and supplication in the Spirit, and watching thereunto with all perseverance and supplication for all saints" (Ephesians 6:18).

Have you considered reading the Bible every day?

The Bible says:

"But his delight is in the law of the LORD; and in his law doth he meditate day and night" (Psalm 1:2).

If you have considered these important issues in your life, you will be a real believer. You will be a good giver to the Lord's work, seeking God's best for your life as you seek to put Him first. You will also be a praying Christian, and you will be a Bible-believing and obeying Christian.

God bless you in these important areas of your life.

Love in Christ,

Pastor _____

# FINANCIAL LETTERS TO HELP CHURCHES

## 7) You Are God's Child

Dear young Christian,

I am writing to you to tell you how happy I am to hear that you have received Jesus Christ as your Lord and Savior. What a thrill to me and to all the people here at _____ Church. You are an answer to our prayers. You are God's child.

You became a child of God when you received Jesus.

"But as many as received him, to them gave he power to become the sons of God, even to them that believe on his name" (John 1:12).

As God's child, you will now want to please Him. There are many ways. They are all found in the Bible. Do what the Bible says, and you will please God. That includes reading His Word and memorizing it:

"Thy word have I hid in mine heart, that I might not sin against thee" (Psalm 119:11).

And if you have a problem with sin, disobeying God, or doing something you ought not do: remember:

"If we confess our sins, he is faithful and just to forgive us our sins, and to cleanse us from all unrighteousness" (1 John 1:9).

As a child of God, may I recommend that you be faithful in church and Sunday School. You will grow there. May I also recommend that you read your Bible and pray every day. Start with the Gospel of John.

As a child of God, may I recommend that you start giving to God's work here in the church. Our gifts help to tell others about Jesus, so they too may receive Him as their Savior. God bless you and keep you.

In Christ,

Pastor _____

## 8) Think Ahead

Dear young friend,

It is wonderful knowing you and having you as a part of our church. Your enthusiasm encourages us. We are glad that you have come to know Jesus personally by receiving Him into your life as your Savior. Our prayer for you is that you will grow in your faith and in your work for Jesus.

We are reminded of a Bible verse:

"Even so faith, if it hath not works, is dead, being alone" (James 2:17).

As we think ahead, as we grow in Him, as we think what we can do for our wonderful Savior, we need to consider these things: We should pray and read our Bible every day. We should be faithful in church attendance and witnessing as well as in our giving.

Another Bible verse to help us is:

"But be ye doers of the word, and not hearers only, deceiving your own selves" (James 1:22).

Praying and reading the Bible isn't only for adults. Attending services and giving isn't only for adults. Telling others about Jesus isn't only for adults either.

Start now: As you think ahead to adulthood, realize that you are preparing for what you will become. Your Christian living now will influence your whole life. Prepare now by living for Jesus, being faithful in God's house, telling others, giving regularly, choosing the right friends, and obeying the Word of God.

Let this Bible verse be your motto: "And whatsoever ye do in word or deed, do all in the name of the Lord Jesus, giving thanks to God and the Father by him" (Colossians 3:17).


In Christian love,


Pastor _____

# FINANCIAL LETTERS TO HELP CHURCHES

## 9) The Bible Tells Me So

Dear young people,

You have often sung the old song: "JESUS LOVES ME! THIS I KNOW, FOR THE BIBLE TELLS ME SO" (Anna B. Warner). And the Bible does tell us so. Be sure to memorize:

"For God so loved the world, that he gave his only begotten Son, that whosoever believeth in him should not perish, but have everlasting life" (John 3:16).

And when you have believed in Him, when you have trusted Jesus as your Lord and Savior, the Bible tells you so many more things: how to live and think and do to please your Savior.

We should love others. The Bible tells me so (1 John 4:7).

We should pray every day. The Bible tells me so (1 Thessalonians 5:17).

We should read and study our Bibles. The Bible tells me so (Psalm 1:2).

We should tell others about Jesus. The Bible tells me so (Acts 1:8).

We should help others. The Bible tells me so (Galatians 6:2).

We should be kind. The Bible tells me so (Ephesians 4:32).

We should give to God's work via our church. The Bible tells me so (Malachi 3:10).

The more you love Jesus, the more you will want to do these things. So remember this letter, remember these and other Bible verses, and do what the Bible says.

God bless you as you grow up loving and serving Jesus.

Pastor _____

## 10) Don't Forget

Dear young friend,

I am so happy to know you and worship with you in church each Sunday.

I am writing today to help you in your Christian life. I want to help you to live for Jesus. And to do so, there are things to remember: things to do, things not to do.

The first step in your Christian life is to know Jesus in a personal way. That comes by receiving Jesus into your heart and life. The Bible says,

"But as many as received him, to them gave he power to become the sons of God, even to them that believe on his name" (John 1:12).

Have you received Him as your Savior? If the answer is no, do it now. If the answer is yes, God wants you to do these things that I suggest.

Don't forget  to pray,
to read your Bible,
to tell others about Jesus,
to be faithful in Sunday School and church,
to give at least 10% (a tithe) of your allowance  or
earnings to Jesus, to be honest, to love everyone,to
help people to be kind, to obeythe Bible.

This is hard when many of your friends don't do these things. This is hard when others make fun of you. This is hard when you don't feel like doing these things. But as you pray and ask for God's help, you can do them. And don't forget, I'm praying for you.

Lovingly in Jesus,


Pastor _____

**"I can do all things through Christ which strengtheneth me"**
**(Philippians 4:13).**

# FINANCIAL LETTERS TO HELP CHURCHES

## 11) The Reason Why

Dear friend in Christ,

You may be young, but you are very important. You may be young, but you can believe in Jesus. You may be young, but you can give to the Lord.

The reason why you are important is that God made you, He sent His Son to die for you, and He has prepared a home in Heaven for you. Therefore, He expects that you will live for Him.

God made you:

"Know ye that the LORD he is God: it is he that hath made us, and not we ourselves; we are his people, and the sheep of his pasture" (Psalm 100:3).

God sent His Son to die for you:

"But God commendeth his love toward us, in that, while we were yet sinners, Christ died for us" (Romans 5:8).

God is preparing a home for us in Heaven:

"In my Father's house are many mansions: if it were not so, I would have told you! I go to prepare a place for you" (John 14:2).

Because of all that God has done for us through Jesus, the least we can do is live for Him and please Him with our lives.

That includes worshiping Him, studying His Word at home alone, and with others in Sunday School, telling others about Him, and sharing what we have with Him.

We share what we have by giving to Him.

"Honour the LORD with thy substance, and with the firstfruits of all thine increase" (Proverbs 3:9).

The reason why we take offerings in our church is to obey God, to give to Him, and to get a blessing as we obey Him. While you are young, start giving to the Lord from what He has given to you.

God will bless you.

Pastor _____

*"...For God loveth a cheerful giver" (2 Corinthians 9:7).*

## 12) Begin Today

Dear _____,

Most people tell you, "Oh, you can't do that until you are older" or "Wait until you grow up."

I want to tell you some things that you can and should do now! You don't have to wait until you grow up. God wants you to do these things now while you are young and throughout your life.

Begin today by believing in Jesus. If you haven't given yourself to Him, do it today:

"...Believe on the Lord Jesus Christ, and thou shalt be saved" (Acts 16:31).

Begin today by obeying His Word: "But be ye doers of the Word, and not hearers only, deceiving your own selves" (James 1:22).

Begin today to give to the Lord's work through your offerings.

"Upon the first day of the week let every one of you lay by him in store, as God hath prospered him, that there be no gatherings when I come" (1 Corinthians 16:2).

If you begin today to live for Jesus, if you begin today to read your Bible and pray, if you begin today to give to God's work, if you begin today to be kind and loving, it will become easier and these good habits will follow you all through your life.

I pray for you.

Sincerely in Christ,


Pastor _____

# CHAPTER SEVEN

# Letters To Far Away Givers

## 1) Greetings From Afar

Dear _____,

Greetings from far away. You are in our hearts and prayers even though you are such a long distance from us. In Christ, the miles melt away and we are as near as a prayer!

What a blessing it is to hear from you and receive your financial gifts for this work. We fondly remember the years you were a part of this church. The miles have separated us, but God has allowed us to be close in fellowship because of the gospel. Thank you for being so generous to the Lord's work here. It is believers like you that help this church to carry on the varied ministries in spite of inflation and difficult times. I think of Philippians 4:16 when I think of your faithfulness in giving to this work of the Lord:

"For even in Thessalonica ye sent once and again unto my necessity." We all praise God for you.

We trust God adds a special blessing to you and your loved ones.

Sincerely in Christ,


Pastor _____

*"We give thanks to God and the Father of our Lord Jesus Christ, praying always for you" (Colossians 1:3).*

## 2) We're Still Serving

Dear friend across the miles,

What a joy it is to keep in touch with you. We fondly remember our many fellowship times in the past, and we praise God for you. You are indeed a blessing from the past and a continued blessing in the present as you pray for this work you left behind when you moved away and as you share in the material needs from time to time.

Each time you send a contribution, it shows us two things:

1) You are still active for the Lord and concerned about His work where you are and around the world, even back to your old church. Thank you.

2) You see that we are still serving here in our community. God is at work here, even as He was when you lived here. He is blessing with people coming to Christ, with young people dedicating their lives to Him, and with church growth and many lives touched.

Your trust in us to put some of God's money into this ministry is a blessing to each and every person in our church. God bless you and continue to use you.


Sincerely in Christ,



Pastor _____




*"Honour the LORD with thy substance, and with the firstfruits of all thine increase" (Proverbs 3:9).*

# FINANCIAL LETTERS TO HELP CHURCHES

## 3) Don't Forget To Pray

Dear friends of _____ Church,

We are so thankful for your continued interest in our church. We praise God for meeting our every need here: through His people, far and near.

We trust that your gifts indicate your continued prayer for the Lord's work in this place. May we suggest several prayer requests we would like you to remember in your quiet time:

1) For the preaching of the Word: that it would be Biblical and applicable to today's Christian living.

2) That our people will reach out to their neighbors and friends and bring them to church.

3) That our missionaries will have strength to carry on in the difficult areas of the world.

4) That petty differences will be left at the cross.

We really appreciate you and trust that if you are ever in this area again, you will worship with us.

God's Word says,

"The liberal soul shall be made fat: and he that watereth shall be watered also himself" (Proverbs 11:25).

God bless you and use you.

Sincerely in our Savior's name,


Pastor _____

## 4) You'll Never Know

Dear friend from afar,

How grateful we are for your friendship, for your interest in our ministry of the gospel, and for your tangible gifts that reveal your love for God and His work.

The Bible reminds us:

"Ye are blessed of the LORD which made heaven and earth" (Psalm 115:15).

"There is that scattereth, and yet increaseth; and there is that withholdeth more than is meet, but it tendeth to poverty" (Proverbs 11:24).

"But this I say, He which soweth sparingly shall reap also sparingly; and he which soweth bountifully shall reapalsobountifully" (2 Corinthians 9:6).

You are very special to me personally and also to the whole body of believers here in this place. Thank you.


In Jesus name,


Pastor _____

# FINANCIAL LETTERS TO HELP CHURCHES

## 5) A Blessing

Dear friend of _____ Church,

Your continued gifts to this church and its ministry here and around the world is a blessing to us as a church and to me as pastor. We can't help but say a big "Thank you."

Your faithfulness in the area of giving draws me to Romans 12 where it says:

"Let love be without dissimulation. Abhor that which is evil; cleave to that which is good. Be kindly affectioned one to another with brotherly love; in honour preferring one another; Not slothful in business; fervent in spirit; serving the Lord; Rejoicing in hope; patient in tribulation; continuing instant in prayer; Distributing to the necessity of saints; given to hospitality" (Romans 12:9-13).

What a blessing you are! Your example in giving, in prayer, and in interest in our church has blessed our people beyond measure. Thank you and may God's blessing be yours each day.


Sincerely in our Savior's name,


Pastor _____

## 6) A Note To Inform You

Dear far away friends,

Your love and care for this fellowship is a real blessing to me and to our entire church. Thank you.

This letter is just a short note to inform you of what we are doing: partially because you, and others like you, continue to give to this ministry.

We have had a successful Vacation Bible School this year with several boys and girls making decisions for Jesus Christ.

We have seen God increase our missionary giving this year, and we have helped missionaries around the world in ten (or 15) countries as well as local ministries.

We have seen a closeness in fellowship that has blessed all our hearts.

We have seen an outreach to the entire community (or troubled youths or divorced, or homeless).

We have seen ten (or ?) come to know Christ as Savior, be baptized, and join our church.

We have seen our Sunday School grow in number as well as depth of Bible study.

Your dollars are working.

You remind us of the verse in 1 Corinthians 4:2:

"Moreover it is required in stewards, that a man be found faithful."

God bless you as you remember this work in your prayers and with your gifts.

Sincerely in Christ,


Pastor _____


*"I thank my God upon every remembrance of you, Always in every prayer of mine for you all making request with joy, For your fellowship in the gospel from the first day until now" (Philippians 1:3-5).*

# FINANCIAL LETTERS TO HELP CHURCHES

## 7) Praise To The Savior

Dear friends,

Praise the Saviour, Ye who know Him!
Who can tell how much we owe Him?
Gladly let us render to Him
All we are and have (Thomas Kelly).

We have so much to praise the Lord for, and you are part of our praise to Him. We praise God for your prayers, for your interest in this work of the Lord, and for your financial gifts.

You have moved away, but you have remembered the blessings and growth in your life from days gone by when you were in our fellowship.

"Praise ye the LORD. Praise the LORD, O my soul. While I live will I praise the LORD: I will sing praises unto my God while I have any being" (Psalm 146:1,2).

We need to praise the Lord that we can give to Him. We need to praise the Lord for what He is doing in our fellowship. We need to praise the Lord for the lives that are being touched. We need to praise the Lord for people that support this work from within our congregation and from afar off. We need to praise the Lord for YOU.

"Praise ye the LORD. Praise ye the LORD from the heavens: praise him in the heights" (Psalm 148:1).

God bless and continue to use you in the days ahead.

In Christian love,


Pastor _____

## 8) You Are Special

Dear friend,

Thank you for your recent contribution to our church. Your love and care of God's people here have proved a blessing and a delight to all of us at _____ Church.

You are special to us because you see a need and help to meet it.

You are special to us because we know you back up your gifts with prayers.

You are special to us because you have not forgotten where you were once nurtured in the Lord.

You are special to us because you keep in touch.

You are special to us because you encourage us in our labors for the Lord.

Thank you. You remind us of Hebrews 3:13:

"But exhort [encourage] one another daily, while it is called to day; lest any of you be hardened through the deceitfulness of sin." Keep up your service to the Lord and His work around the world.


Lovingly,


Pastor _____

# FINANCIAL LETTERS TO HELP CHURCHES

## 9) We Hear...

Dear friend of _____ Church,

Greetings in the name of the Lord Jesus Christ. It is wonderful to remember our former fellowship times. And now that you are far away, it is great that you remember us back home!

We hear...that you are still trusting the Lord.

We hear...that you are doing well in your work (or school).

We hear...that you miss this fellowship.

We hear...that you send some of the Lord's money back here to meet needs as they arise. Praise the Lord. We are so thankful for your concern and tangible evidence of it.

"By him therefore let us offer the sacrifice of praise to God continually, that is, the fruit of our lips giving thanks to his name. But to do good and to communicate forget not: for with such sacrifices God is well pleased" (Hebrews 13:15,16).

God bless you and continue to use you.

In Christian love,



Pastor _____

*"Rejoice evermore. Pray without ceasing. In every thing give thanks: for this is the will of God in Christ Jesus concerning you" (1 Thessalonians 5:16-18).*

## 10) God's Added Blessings

Dear friend across the miles,

God is so good. He adds blessing upon blessing.

"Blessed is the man whose strength is in thee" (Psalm 84:5a).

"Praise ye the LORD. Blessed is the man that feareth the LORD, that delighteth greatly in his commandments. He shall not be afraid of evil tidings: his heart is fixed, trusting in the LORD" (Psalm 112:1,7).

When we do God's work, He showers blessings on us. When we give to God, He gives more. We thank you for your remembrances of this church with your generous gifts from time to time. We see in Malachi 3:10 that His blessings in giving tithes into the storehouse result in more blessings than we have room to receive! Your offerings, above your storehouse tithing, to your former church body, increases your blessing and your influence for the gospel of Christ. All we who tithe and give an offering have experienced God's added blessings.

Your dedication to the Lord and His work here is an added blessing to us and enables us to expand the work. We thank you in Jesus' name.

God is using your gift in adding equipment to our Sunday School (or buying new hymn books, paying bills, painting the ceiling, or ?). We constantly praise God for you, and others like you, who remember this mission field.

In Christian love across the miles,

Pastor _____

*"Praise ye the LORD. Praise God in his sanctuary: praise him in the firmament of his power. Let every thing that hath breath praise the LORD. Praise ye the LORD" (Psalm 150:1,6).*

# FINANCIAL LETTERS TO HELP CHURCHES

## 11) Sincere Thanks

Dear contributor,

Some people never say, "Thank you." Remember the story of the ten lepers who were healed. Only one said "thank you."

"And one of them, when he saw that he was healed, turned back, and with a loud voice glorified God, And fell down on his face at his feet, giving him thanks: and he was a Samaritan. And Jesus answering said, Were there not ten cleansed? but where are the nine? (Luke 17:15-17).

Some people say "thank you" in a flip, unmeaningful way and don't mean it. They just say the polite words, but their heart is not in it.

BUT: We say a sincere, heartfelt, honest "T H A N K   Y O U" to someone who has blessed our hearts and our lives. You have not forgotten us! Your gift has been put to good use, and our people are encouraged by your generosity.

We say with the psalmist:

"Wait on the LORD: be of good courage, and he shall strengthen thine heart: wait, I say, on the LORD" (Psalm 27:14).

And "Give unto the LORD the glory due unto his name; worship the LORD in the beauty of holiness" (Psalm 29:2).

Thank you for helping us to praise the Lord and give glory to Him. Your giving is part of your worship, and together we have worshiped God in the beauty of holiness.

God bless you and continue to use you.

Sincerely in Christ,



Pastor _____

## 12) Keep In Touch

Dear ones,

Greetings from _____ Church.

We think of Philippians 1:4-6 when we think of you:

"Always in every prayer of mine for you all making request with joy, For your fellowship in the gospel from the first day until now; Being confident of this very thing, that he which hath begun a good work in you will perform it until the day of Jesus Christ."

We are so happy to hear from you. We are thrilled to know you are living for the Lord and loving and serving Him. Keep in touch. We can pray for you more intelligently when you write and share with us.

We praise God for using this church to reach out into our community. God has enabled us to bring people to Himself and to encourage the believers in their Christian walk. Your support of this work helps in that calling.

Thank you. If there is any way we can help you, be sure to let us know. Let us hear from you again...keep in touch.


In Christian love,


Pastor _____


*"Be kindly affectioned one to another with brotherly love; in honour preferring one another. Distributing to the necessity of saints; given to hospitality" (Romans 12:10,13)*

# CHAPTER EIGHT

# Letters To Makers Of Wills

## 1) The Law Says

Dear _____,

I am writing to you dear people in our fellowship to help you make the right decision about your financial future. How important it is to think ahead. I am referring to the writing of a will.

We all may think that is something for the rich and famous to do. But be aware; we will all die and we will all have some possessions to dispose of, small or great.

Without a properly negotiated will, the law says that money has to go the way it directs, no matter what the deceased person's desire is.

We must be willing to care for our own in our wills. We must see to it that our loved ones will receive their due share if, or rather when, the Lord calls us home.

But let us not stop there. Consider giving something to the Lord's work from your accumulated wealth. It could be a tenth of your estate, it could be what is in a certain savings account, or it could be the money from one of your life insurance policies. But should not God's people remember their loving Savior at the time they go home to be with the Lord? You can no longer use your money, nor can you take it with you. The family can't or won't give what you might think of giving without it being in black and white in your personal will.

Please, take this letter seriously and write your will. Take care of your family and take care of your church family. God bless you as you consider these suggestions. If I can be of any help in the process, please let me know. I would be glad to introduce you to a Christian lawyer or a financial counselor.

God bless you and use you each day of your life.

Sincerely,


Pastor _____

*"For to me to live is Christ, and to die is gain" (Philippians 1:21).*

# FINANCIAL LETTERS TO HELP CHURCHES

## *2) We Must*

Dear ones in our special fellowship,

"Lay not up for yourselves treasures upon earth, where moth and rust doeth corrupt, and where thieves break through and steal: But lay up for yourselves treasures in heaven, where neither moth nor rust doth corrupt, and where thieves do not break through nor steal" (Matthew 6:19,20).

These verses make us think of giving: via our local church, missions program, or via our last will and testament.

We would rather think of life than of death. It is easy to think we will live forever here on earth rather than in Heaven. But the Bible indicates that, unless the Lord comes back beforehand, we must all die physically. Those of us who have received the Lord Jesus into our lives as Lord and Savior will live forever with Him.

But WE MUST think about our own "home-going" because if God calls us, then our family, our church, and our favorite Christian organizations will need some of our continued support.

We ought, we should, WE MUST take time while we are in our sound mind to write a God-honoring will. If we now give ten percent of our income to the Lord, why not leave ten percent of our estate to the Lord? It must be done legally, via a properly executed will and last testament. If we would like a gift to go to some organization of our denomination, the time to plan that is NOW. So, if you haven't already, don't let another day go by without writing your will to provide for your loved ones and for your beloved church and denomination.

God bless you in this endeavor.

Sincerely in Christ,

Pastor _____

*"For where your treasure is, there will your heart be also"*
*(Matthew 6:21).*

## 3) Some Wait Too Long

Dear ones in Christ,

You are a very special part of our fellowship. God has been good to bring people like you into _____ Church. Your life and testimony are a blessing to me personally and to all the body of believers here in our church.

I am writing today, not just to you, but to all those who love the Lord and seek to serve Him, to inquire about your estate, the making of your will. You probably have already taken care of such an undertaking, but because I read recently that 70 percent of all people die without a will, I thought I had better share a little information with you at this time.

Most of us don't like to think of death, but it comes to everyone, whether they are ready or not. We have thoughts of giving to our families, of giving to the Lord's work, of being a blessing after death, as we have been during life.

But, without a will, nothing will go to the Lord's work. Our desires for family members will not be fulfilled, but will be decided by the state in which we reside.

If our people left a tenth of their estate to the Lord's work, what great things the churches educational and missions organizations would be able to accomplish. Pray, make an appointment with a lawyer, talk to some Christian with know-how in this field, and take care of this task before it is too late. Very seldom will a deathbed will stand up in court.

Thank you for reading this and praise God, you either have already heeded its warning or you will do it very soon. Remember, too many wait too long!

Sincerely in Christ,

Pastor _____

*"I have shewed you all things, how that so labouring ye ought to support the weak, and to remember the words of the Lord Jesus, how he said, It is more blessed to give than to receive" (Acts 20:35).*

# 4) Check The Word

Dear loved one in the Lord,

Greetings in the name of our Lord Jesus Christ. He is so wonderful: He goes with us wherever we go, for He said:

"...FOR THE LORD THY GOD IS WITH THEE WHITHERSO-EVER THOU GOEST" (Joshua 1:9).

Many people would rather not think about what I will discuss in this letter. They think the inevitable will never happen; but remember, God says:

"So teach us to number our days, that we may apply our hearts unto wisdom" (Psalm 90:12).

My purpose in writing to you today is to encourage you to make a will, if you have not done so already. A last will and testament is essential to fairly care for your family and for your other desires, including your Christian concerns. The state will divide your money among blood relatives without a will; but there, positively, could not be any gifts to your beloved church or denominational organizations.

The Bible says:

"...Thus saith the LORD, Set thine house in order: for thou shalt die, and not live" (Isaiah 38:1). A true translation of that Hebrew means: make a will. The Bible also says:

"But if any provide not for his own, and specially for those of his own house, he hath denied the faith, and is worse than an infidel" (1 Timothy 5:8).

Place God's Word, the Bible, in your hands, in your mind, and in your heart. How can you do less than give Him your best in life and in death?

I would love to encourage and help you with your will: choosing a lawyer, deciding on how to divide your estate, and the desire to be prepared. I am not interested in any personal gain, only to suggest making a Christian will. If there is anything I can do for you in this area, please call me at _____ .

Sincerely,

Pastor _____

# FINANCIAL LETTERS TO HELP CHURCHES

## 5) Keep On Giving

Dear ones at _____ Church,

We love you in the Lord. We pray for you. We are concerned about you and your home life, your church life, and your work life. We even care about your stewardship. You give regularly to the ministry here at _____ Church. Thank you.

We would like to ask you to give forever, but there is a terminus for all of us. The day will come, if Jesus doesn't come first, when each of us will die; and praise the Lord, we who know and love Jesus will go to be with Him forever and ever.

Giving is a blessing and a privilege for those who know and trust the Lord. The Bible says,

"It is more blessed to give than to receive" (Acts 20:36b).

But as "The death dew lies cold on my brow" (A.J. Gordon, "My Jesus, I Love Thee"), our giving days will be over. There will be no more collection plates and no more opportunities to share our resources with Bible-believing churches and organizations.

But there is a way to give after your committal service. Via advance planning, a properly executed will can provide an inheritance for your church of whatever amount you desire.

Not many plan ahead and few consider leaving some of their estate to their church where they have worshiped and served for many years.

Remember Matthew 6:33:

"But seek ye first the kingdom of God, and his righteousness; and all these things shall be added unto you."

If we do that with the making of our will, we can KEEP ON GIV-ING after we have gone "home" to be with the Lord. Those who are left behind will continue to be blessed by our generosity. And, we pray, some will come to know Christ and join us in Heaven because of our gifts. It could and it should happen.

Consider these thoughts seriously. And if I can be of any help, let me know.

Your Pastor _____

## 6) It's Easy

Dear ones,

It is so special to know you and worship with you. You are close to our hearts and in our daily prayers.

"First, I thank my God through Jesus Christ for you all, that your faith is spoken of throughout the whole world" (Romans 1:8).

Yes, our missionary friends around the world are thankful for your faith. Other churches know of your faith. And I do thank God for you as Paul did for the Romans.

You are faithful givers to the Lord's work here in our community and around the world. Oh, that people like you could go on forever with your faithfulness!

But God intends to take us home to be with Him in due time. And we agree with Paul who wrote:

"We are confident, I say, and willing rather to be absent from the body, and to be present with the Lord" (2 Corinthians 5:8).

Do you realize you can be faithful in gifts after you leave this world and go to be with Jesus? And IT'S as EASY as A-B-C.

A) Ask God for wisdom in writing a will that pleases Him. Do not neglect your family, but consider a portion of your estate to go to the Lord's work. B) Begin today. Delay can only make it impossible. Tomorrow may not come! C) Go to a lawyer and make the will legal to ensure your wishes are followed.

Young people need to write a will to be sure their children are cared for (via guardianship) in case of an accident or illness that would claim both parents.

Middle-aged people need a will, even if they don't think they have very much. An insurance policy could bring thousands of dollars into an estate. And, of course, older people, even with limited resources, need a

# FINANCIAL LETTERS TO HELP CHURCHES

109

will. Please, consider this important task now! It's not difficult. IT'S as EASY as A-B-C. If I can help, please give me a call.

Sincerely in Christ,

Pastor _____

*"For with God nothing shall be impossible" (Luke 1:37).*

## 7) Neglect Not Your Family

Dear Christian family,

We love you in the Lord. We are in the business of helping people, and we feel like we have a matter to discuss with all the body of believers here at _____ Church.

We are shocked when we read that one-third of all New York people die without a will (Wall Street Journal, October 27, 1980). That statistic is similar all around our country. We are further shocked when we discover that Christians are as guilty as non-Christians. Get busy: write your will.

Do not leave everything to the church unless you have no family, or your family is so well taken care of that they insist. The Bible tells us:

"But if any provide not for his own, and specially for those of his own house, he hath denied the faith, and is worse than an infidel" (1 Timothy 5:8).

Provide for guardianship of young children; provide a trust for those not capable of handling finances; provide cash for spouse to live on. Be sure to provide. Yes, you can give a sum to the church. A good guideline might be a tithe of your estate. Remember the words of Scripture in 1 Timothy 5:8. You are responsible to God.

Write your will today. Get it legal via a lawyer. Praise God that you are willing to listen.


Sincerely in Christ,


Pastor _____


> **"And whatsoever ye do in word or deed, do all in the name of the Lord Jesus, giving thanks to God and the father by him"**
> **(Colossians 3:17).**

# 8) Neglect Not God's Work

Dear ones in Christ,

Recently I wrote a letter to you to suggest that you write a will that would provide for your family, if you were called home to be with the Lord. How important that is. Remember 1 Timothy 5:8.

However, usually the problem is not on neglecting the family. Most people seem to feel it is their obligation to give all that they have to the family. They want their children and grandchildren to remember them, and money and property are one way to get them to "not forget you."

However, the Bible tells us to put first things first (Matthew 6:33). Psalm 37:25 tells us,

"I have been young, and now am old; yet have I not seen the righteous forsaken, nor his seed begging bread."

God is so good. Trust Him in this life and in the life to come. Trust Him with your salary now; trust Him with your estate in the days to come. Remember Him with a portion of each paycheck; remember Him with a portion of your estate after you are gone. That will help the Lord's work to continue. You will receive a blessing in this life, and your church and your missionaries will continue to minister after God calls you home.

When you make provision for your church in a will, you are truly writing a Christian will. But your desires will not be fulfilled in death if they are not spelled out in a legal will.

Some say, I don't have enough money or assets to give to the Lord. I love the hymn by Kitty J. Suffield: "Little is much when God is in it! Labor not for wealth or fame; There's a crown and you can win it, If you'll go in Jesus' name." Your little and my little add up to much for God's work.

"Bear ye one another's burdens, and so fulfil the law of Christ" (Galatians 6:2).

In Christian love,

Pastor _____

*"We then that are strong ought to bear the infirmities of the weak, and not to please ourselves" (Romans 15:1).*

# FINANCIAL LETTERS TO HELP CHURCHES

## 9) Consider Others

Dear members and friends of _____ Church,

I love to write letters, but this letter is not easy to write. People are sensitive about the subject. You see, I'm writing about making a will, or rewriting a will! Have you written yours? If the answer is "no," isn't it time you did? If the answer is "yes," isn't it time to update it to meet your family situation as of today?

And, in either situation, have you considered others in your will? "What?" you ask. "Others besides my family?" Yes, have you considered others? And I mean your church family and your missionary family. Do you realize that you have received an inheritance from God?

"Knowing that of the Lord ye shall receive the reward of the inheritance: for ye serve the Lord Christ" (Colossians 3:24). And the Lord is interested in our inheritance. He doesn't need our money,

"For every beast of the forest is mine, and the cattle upon a thousand hills" (Psalm 50:10). But God goes on in that Psalm to tell us,

"Offer unto God thanksgiving; and pay thy vows unto the most high."

One way to do that is to put God's work into our will. Consider a gift to your church from your estate, to the missionary budget, to the building fund, to the benevolent fund, or a gift to our denomination.

Yes, I recommend that you place God's work in your will, so you will be able to keep on giving after you have gone home to be with the Lord. But if you just think about it, it won't happen; if you just plan to do it, it won't happen. Only if you write it into your will and have it legally drawn up, will it occur. If you plan to do it, praise the Lord and get busy. If you aren't convinced, please pray about the matter and act soon.

Sincerely in our Savior's name,

Pastor _____ and the finance committee

*"...Not my will, but thine, be done" (Luke 22:42).*

## 10) It's Possible

Dear ones in Christ,

It's possible. It's possible to live for Christ in this wicked world. Philippians 4:13: "I can do all things through Christ which strengtheneth me."

It's possible to speak to others about Christ in this wicked world. Acts 1:8 declares:

"But ye shall receive power, after that the Holy Ghost is come upon you: and ye shall be witnesses...."

It's possible to praise God in every circumstance. Psalm 34:1 helps us:

"I will bless the LORD at all times: his praise shall continually be in my mouth."

It is possible to make a "Christ-honoring will." Perhaps you are saying: My little isn't worth bothering with!

or: I'm too busy! I'm not going to die yet! It is too costly!

or: Nobody else is doing it!

or: Wills are just another money-making scheme for lawyers!

or: I plan to do it next week! I'm too young!

But God isn't interested in our excuses, for He says,

"For with God nothing shall be impossible" (Luke 1:37).

Why not start the process right now? Provide for your family from whatever money you leave behind.

Provide for your church from whatever money you leave behind.

"Every man shall give as he is able, according to the blessing of the LORD thy God which he hath given thee" (Deuteronomy 16:17).

Therefore, I declare to you, in Christian love, it is possible, it is necessary, it is your duty to write a will that provides for both your family and the Lord's work. Won't you do it today?

Sincerely in Christian love,

Pastor _____

# FINANCIAL LETTERS TO HELP CHURCHES

## 11) Not Just The Wealthy

Dear members of friends,

How we appreciate your faithful giving to our church. Your gifts make it possible for us to keep this ministry going and to give toward the missionary needs around the world.

God is so good. He has planned for all people: those with lots of money, those with little. No matter what our income, God has a fair way for us to give: it is the tithing method. Some give more; some give less. But God suggests a tithe and an offering.

And as I look to the future, I realize that all of us will someday be unable to give. We will go to be with the Lord, which is far better. But on that day, will our tithes and offerings cease also?

It need not happen. If we plan ahead, if we make sure we write our will, if we remember God's work in our will, if we perhaps tithe our estate, our gifts will go on after our death.

We are burdened now for God's work. But the majority of people I talk with haven't made a will. And many of the people who have made a will have not included the church. Let me challenge you: Give God a tithe or some portion of your estate. You will be with your beloved Savior, but your ability to reach other souls for Christ will continue.

But you say you haven't got much. Be assured, you don't have to be wealthy. Just look at this imaginary chart: as different people, with different sizes of estates, would turn their assets into a goodly sum:

| | | | | | |
|---|---|---|---|---|---|
| Mr. A: | with an estate of | $125,000 | –tithe | = | $12,500 |
| Miss. B: | with an estate of | $200,000 | –tithe | = | $20,000 |
| Mr. C: | with an estate of | $ 18,000 | –tithe | = | $ 1,800 |
| Mr. D: | with an estate of | $ 46,230 | –tithe | = | $ 4,623 |
| Mrs. E: | with an estate of | $250,000 | –tithe | = | $25,000 |
| Miss F: | with an estate of | $ 4300 | –tithe | = | $ 430 |
| Mr. G: | with an estate of | $ 56,150 | –tithe | = | $ 5,615 |
| Mrs. H: | with an estate of | $ 24,600 | –tithe | = | $ 2,460 |
| Mr. I: | with an estate of | $ 110,000 | –tithe | = | $11,000 |
| Miss J: | with an estate of | $ 10,400 | –tithe | = | $ 1,040 |

Local church, missions, and/or Christian education would get: $84,468.

If that is your desire, it must be written into your will. It will please the Lord, it will please the church, and it will please you. Don't wait until you are wealthy: do it NOW! The Bible says:

"Let all things be done decently and in order" (1 Corinthians 14:40).

Please pray about this matter of a will and ask God to help you write a will that will please Him. Settle this matter soon.

In prayerful concern,

Pastor _____

# FINANCIAL LETTERS TO HELP CHURCHES

## 12) Me?

Dear people of God,

Our God is good. He is kind and compassionate. And He desires that we live for Him and be like His Son, Jesus.

"Therefore, my beloved brethren, be ye stedfast, unmoveable, always abounding in the work of the Lord, forasmuch as ye know that your labour is not in vain in the Lord" (1 Corinthians 15:58).

If only we would memorize and practice that verse. It would help us in every circumstance of life.

It would help me; it would help you. It is imperative that we plan our giving to God in a dedicated fashion. You already give to the Lord's work here in our fellowship. How we appreciate your prayers and gifts to keep this ministry going forward. We could all do more, but we praise God for what we are doing and what we will do in the future.

But there will come a day when we can no longer give. When we go home to be with the Lord, our giving will stop. Or will it? It depends on what you do now as to what will happen with your accumulated wealth and properties.

What about giving a tithe or more of your estate to God's work? It is possible and it would still assure your family of having a good portion of your money and property. "But," you say, "ME? I can't do that. It belongs to my children and grandchildren. ME? I shouldn't worry about the future. First of all, I have very little to leave in an estate. And second, my children would need a little extra when I'm gone. Count me out!"

"ME?" Yes, YOU! Because Proverbs 22:9 says:

"He that hath a bountiful eye shall be blessed; for he giveth of his bread to the poor."

"ME?" Yes, YOU! Because 2 Corinthians 9:6 says:

"But this I say, he which soweth sparingly shall reap also sparingly; and he which soweth bountifully shall reap also bountifully."

"ME?" Yes, YOU! Because 2 Corinthians 9:7 says:

"Every man according as he purposeth in his heart, so let him give;

not grudgingly, or of necessity: for God loveth a cheerful giver."

I may not dictate to you to give; I cannot force you to write a will and to include God's work in that will. But I can strongly suggest it and I can pray that you will heed my advice. The blessing will be yours in this life and in the next for the Bible teaches us:

"Lay not up for yourselves treasures upon earth, where moth and rust doth corrupt, and where thieves break through and steal: but lay up for yourselves treasures in heaven, where neither moth nor rust doth corrupt, and where thieves do not break through nor steal: For where your treasure is, there will your heart be also" (Matthew 6:19-21).

Thanks for reading this special letter. It is not meant to antagonize you. Please take it in the spirit it is written. Share your response with me sometime.

God bless you.

Sincerely in Christ,


Pastor _____

# CONCLUSION

These letters are prepared for the pastor, for the finance committee (and under their direction), and/or for the church secretary to write and mail to people in these different categories.

We need to instruct our people to tithe and given an offering.

We need to educate our people to help with the building fund.

We need to teach our people to give more to missions.

We need to teach our people to give to the total denominational program.

We need to coach our people to practice "storehouse" tithing.

We need to encourage people who used to give but have slackened in their gifts. We need to guide our young people, our future givers.

We need to thank and inspire those who have moved away (our far-away givers). We need to advise our people about making a will and including God's work in their will.

As we teach our people from the Scriptures, we can help them realize what the Bible teaches:

"Therefore to him that knoweth to do good, and doeth it not, to him it is sin" (James 4:17).

The suggestions are provided. Perhaps the letters will need to be altered slightly to meet a particular need; perhaps the letters can add a personal greeting; perhaps the letters can be sent just as they are written. But write to the people and see God work through your letters. The gifts will increase and the needs will be met if you don't beg for money, if you don't down-grade the people for not giving. Try to encourage and instruct in a loving and Scriptural manner.

May God use you and your ministry via *Financial Letters To Help Churches.*

*"If ye love me, keep my commandments" (John 14:15).*